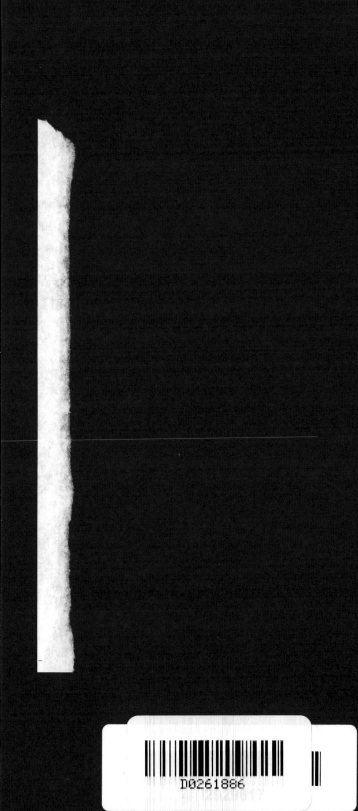

my hero THEO

my hero THEO

The brave police dog who went beyond the call of duty to save lives

GARETH GREAVES

HARPER
element

Certain details, including names, places and dates,
have been changed to protect privacy.

HarperElement
An imprint of HarperCollins*Publishers*
1 London Bridge Street
London SE1 9GF

www.harpercollins.co.uk

First published by HarperElement 2020

1 3 5 7 9 10 8 6 4 2

© Gareth Greaves 2020

Plate-section images courtesy of the author

Gareth Greaves asserts the moral right to
be identified as the author of this work

A catalogue record of this book is
available from the British Library

ISBN 978-0-00-838522-4

Printed and bound in Great Britain by
CPI Group (UK) Ltd, Croydon

MIX
Paper from
responsible sources
FSC™ C007454

This book is produced from independently certified FSC™ paper
to ensure responsible forest management.

For more information visit: www.harpercollins.co.uk/green

For Ben:
Thank you for teaching me to be a dad.
You've shown me what true bravery means

For Eryn, my Little Bird:
Fly high, dream big and stay brave. I love
you more than you'll ever know

For Theo:
I'd give the world to work alongside
you again. I'd follow your paws until I could
follow no more. You gave me hope and a future.
I owe you more than I can ever give you,
now it's my turn to look after you.
State 11, son

PROLOGUE

SCREAMING FOR BACKUP was hopeless. My radio was within reaching distance, near a drain by the kerb, but rather than reach for it and issue the familiar '6143, urgent!' shout, I was trying desperately to stop Theo's neck from snapping.

'Bite him, George, bite his ear off …'

They weren't talking about me.

Minutes earlier, the two men I was trying to subdue had been driving at 90mph in a car they'd just stolen. A high-speed pursuit ended with them abandoning the vehicle and making off on foot. Their attempt to escape had come to a swift end when Theo, my five-year-old German Shepherd police dog, chased them from their abandoned car through an urban housing estate in Manchester and cornered them. On my command, he'd bitten one on the arm, which usually signalled the end of the altercation and the start of an arrest – not this time, though.

Theo had gripped his arm but, high on drugs, George Marshall had wrestled him into a headlock and was bent double, using all his weight trying to break Theo's neck. Theo didn't whimper or release his grip when I heard the stomach-churning sound of cartilage being ripped in two as his ear was bitten right through.

Seeing him dripping with blood, I raised my knee with all the force I could straight into Marshall's face, making sure I missed Theo completely and hoping it'd make him release or at least loosen his grip.

It worked how I intended and Theo was free. I knew he wouldn't leave me but while I tried to subdue the man who'd tried to kill my dog, he swung at me and split my lip wide open. Both of us now covered in blood, I wrestled him into a headlock. All I could hear were a series of deafening thuds and all I could feel was Marshall's body rocking back and forth as I fought to detain him. I knew he was kicking Theo as hard as he could and later, I'd find out the kicks badly bruised several of Theo's thirteen ribs. Still not a sound from Theo while we battled on for minutes in the fight of our lives. When help finally arrived, we were exhausted.

Leaving other officers to make the arrest, I patched

Theo up, washing his wounds with a bottle of water I had in the van. I used the doggy first aid bag I always carry in the van to stem the blood while I called the emergency vet, letting them know we were on our way. My own split lip stung as I spoke, the dried blood cracking as I explained his injuries. When I hung up, Theo licked my hands and gently nuzzled my leg while he whimpered in pain.

Exhausted and sore, I crouched down to his level, then sat and leant against the police van. He rested his head against me and at exactly the same moment we let out the same long, low sigh.

'I'm sorry, son. You alright?'

I avoided his ear which had stopped bleeding and used the bottle of water to try and rinse some of his bright red blood from his head. I could see he couldn't lie down, it was clear he was in pain, so I gently helped him up into the van and we drove to the vet. While he was being patched up, I ran through what had happened in my head.

I'd never trained him to stay and fight if I was in trouble. Dogs have a natural self-preservation instinct; it's been in them for thousands of years and has ensured they survive as a species. Anyone with a dog will know they rarely get themselves into a scrape they can't get out of. Every fibre in him must have wanted to run off, but he stayed and took a battering because in addition to self-preservation, German Shepherd dogs have a huge loyalty gene: when they love you, they'll never leave you.

I hadn't once trained Theo to override that natural instinct, but he had and I guessed I was still standing because of it.

He hadn't known not to whimper and he must have been in excruciating pain. Dogs have three nerve centres on their bodies and one of them is their ears – it must have been agony when it was bitten and when his ribs broke, but he'd ignored the pain and undoubtedly saved my life in the process.

We'd been in some scrapes together up to that point and we'd be in many more to come, but replaying what had just happened to us both, I knew I'd never work with a police dog like Theo ever again. Looking into those big brown eyes while he was fixed by the vet, I got goosebumps. His eyes are the most beautiful of any dog I've ever seen and when we look at each other, it's like we connect on an incredible level, a bond that can't be put into words.

I didn't need to thank him more than I had. He understood. Our bond became unbreakable at that moment. We'd both fought for our lives but hadn't even considered leaving each other's side. We weren't a handler and a dog, we were one.

Manpol Theo,* my boy, my son.

* Police dogs owned by the Greater Manchester Police Force are referred to as 'Manpol', a shortening of Manchester Police. Each force across the country has its own version of the name – for example, Merseyside Police Force dogs are called Merpol.

1

I GREW UP IN A PLACE called Clayton in Manchester. It was a really rough estate with plenty of crime and neglect. Kids left school at fifteen with few prospects and half of them there lived in poverty. Dad was a coach driver and Mum was a part-time cleaner. I'm the third of four and we had a tough childhood. Times were tight and, to put it bluntly, we had sod all! Mum wanted the best for us, though, and from when we were tiny she was adamant she wanted us all to go to private school. Fees aren't cheap and Dad worked long hours to afford it for us. He'd take any overtime he could on evenings and weekends, determined we'd have a better shot of making it in life than he'd had.

My older brother Janade, younger brother Gavin and older sister Suzanne all happily toed the family line and enjoyed a private education at St Bede's College in

Whalley Range, Manchester, with Latin lessons and access to sport, but I refused point-blank to go. Despite my protestations, Mum and Dad insisted that I at least sit the entrance exam. I dutifully agreed to this, then spent the next ninety minutes refusing to even write my name down on the piece of paper. They went mad when a teacher told them what I'd done but I didn't want to follow the same path as my siblings; it didn't interest me. Being the stubborn child I was, I attended the local primary and comp while my siblings were carted off in their posh uniforms every day.

I always had an affinity with dogs and knew from a really young age I wanted to be a police dog handler so it seemed pointless to go to private school when I knew I didn't need degrees or exams to join up and apply to the Police Dog Unit. I'd seen plenty of dog handlers on our estate when a family row had got out of hand or a stolen car had been dumped. I'd watch intently as the handlers would let the dogs get a scent then give them space to work. They seemed so in tune, not a dog and a human working together but one unit, one entity. It was fascinating and I loved watching them from my bedroom window on the occasions they'd be on the estate.

My two brothers and I shared a room and my sister had one to herself, which never seemed fair, but that didn't change, no matter how much we boys protested.

Mum and Dad were like all the other working-class parents on the estate; theirs wasn't the happiest of marriages. I remember arguments and rows over money, but rather than let it affect me, I was in my own happy world with Rufus.

I was four years old when Rufus first came into my world. He was imaginary but that didn't matter. He was a mongrel, and Mum and Dad would ask what he was but the best my four-year-old mind could manage was to describe him as 'a gingery dog'. I can still picture him now, though, and these days he'd be a Spaniel cross with shaggy ears. He was lovely and was my best friend. He never came out, he was only ever in the house, but I needed that dog so much. I'd talk to him about everything, spend hours playing with him and training him, and he never left my side.

Rufus soon made way for Cindy – a real dog – when I was around seven years old. A little grey Staffie, she had the loveliest temperament. She belonged to a neighbour, but I'd ask if I could walk her, such was my obsession with these four-legged creatures. Our neighbour agreed and soon enough Cindy started showing up outside our house a few minutes before it was time for us to go for a walk. Her dedication to me continued and the more affection I showed her, the more she showed me. I'd fuss her and give her treats, and while she'd always had the softest nature, if Mum or Dad were shouting at me then she'd start to growl at them. Eventually, Mum made me swear I'd stop spending time with Cindy in the hope her protectiveness towards me would wear off, but we were a unit until my parents moved house half a mile down the road when I was ten and I couldn't see her anymore.

While I missed Cindy massively, Denver came along when I was around thirteen. Denver was a Rottweiler cross. I found him in the street and he had mange, a skin disease caused by parasites. I can't remember when I first saw him and no one in our neighbourhood ever knew who he belonged to, so I'd feed him and he started to follow me around. He'd come in the garden and Mum would swear, shouting that the 'scabby-looking thing' wasn't allowed in the house, but little by little, as he wormed his way into my affections, I could also see him worming his way into Mum's. With hindsight, I'll admit he was absolutely gross, but he was my first living and breathing dog that belonged to me and I loved every single thing about him.

Denver must have been a few months old when he came to live with us permanently and while Mum and

Dad were at first utterly against me having him, I was undeterred. After ongoing negotiations, we reached a compromise, agreeing that Denver would live outside and not be allowed in the house. He was my first experience of having a pet and he was hilarious.

What Mum didn't know was that whenever she was out, I'd sneak Denver inside and upstairs to my bedroom. Like most families, we had routines and every Saturday my brothers, sister and I would have to help Mum clean the house from top to bottom and change all the beds. She'd put her Billy Joel album on the record player and we'd all muck in together to get it done faster. I was stripping the beds upstairs one Saturday with the melancholic tones of 'Piano Man' ringing up the stairs. Mum had popped to the shops to get something and I'd let Denver in while I finished cleaning. He was being really quiet and, suspecting he might be up to something, I went out onto the landing to see where he was.

I set foot out of the bedroom in time to see the final few white feathers cascading like snowflakes onto the hall landing. He'd grabbed one of the pillows from Mum and Dad's bed and had wrestled with it, completely destroying it. The entire landing was covered in white feathers. It looked like a down factory and in the middle stood a triumphant Denver, breathless and wagging his tail, proud of his accomplishment and expecting me to share in his joy. When she got back, Mum was understandably livid and turfed him out of the house, saying he was never, ever allowed to cross the threshold again.

Denver's destructive streak continued unabated, though, whether it was snaffling food off the kitchen counter or eating homework – yes, really, he had the most lovable nature but couldn't resist a nibble and a play. By the time I was in Fourth Year, I was 80 per cent absent from school because of that dog. Denver's traits had made a rod for his own back and he was definitely an outdoor dog after Mum lost one too many things due to his exuberance. He had a kennel but I desperately wanted him in the house with me.

I'd get on the bus to go to school because Dad was the bus driver but then I'd dash home and spend the day in the house with Denver, sharing cups of tea and biscuits with him. I couldn't cope with him being outside all day on his own so I'd go home and keep him company.

Despite the fact the internet didn't exist in those days, and I had no clue what I was doing, I'd spend hours training Denver. I was starting from scratch and, by trial and error, we got to a point where I could walk him to the shop off the lead to get something for Mum and he'd stay by my side and wait patiently outside while I went in and got what was needed.

I didn't like him crossing roads so I'd walk him to the main road. I then had to cross and get him to sit and wait. I'd cross over and go through a 30-metre alleyway, get what I needed and he'd wait for me. He couldn't see me and I wasn't in his line of sight, but he trusted me to come back and I'd trained him to trust me. I was so proud of how responsive he was – I didn't know back then how accomplished that was for both of us. I didn't need to put him on a lead. If I had done, he'd probably have taken me off my feet – I was never exactly a strapping lad – but he'd do what I asked and a mutual respect grew between us.

Being a handler and owner isn't about power and owning an animal, it's about a mutual respect and good treatment. How could I expect Denver or any other dog to do as I wanted if I didn't treat him well and praise his successes? I didn't know it at the time but when I joined the Dog Unit, a lot of those lessons I'd taught myself came back to me. No dog will do what you tell it to do if it's not respected. I might be Theo's handler, but we're very much a team in the way Denver and I were.

I spent many of my formative years obsessed with a fairly mangy mongrel as my peer group were getting up to all sorts and Denver was my escape. On our walks, we'd often go past the police station and so my fascination with dog handlers grew. I'd see them coming on or off shift and they looked so commanding. Spending time with Denver was my favourite thing to do and it seemed these men and women got to spend their working lives with dogs – they didn't just have them as pets at home. It seemed such an appealing path to follow.

I left secondary school with a handful of GCSEs intent on being a dog handler, but at sixteen I was too young to join the police so I started out as a maintenance apprentice at a health club in Manchester. Denver finally became an indoor dog when I earned enough money to rent a little place for the two of us near work.

My fascination with the police force continued, though. Mum and Dad had done everything they could to give us kids a leg-up and get us a successful career but they didn't have the money for us to fall back on. They had love and food on the table, but I knew when I got my first job I'd be financially responsible for myself for the rest of my life. I wanted a financial stability my parents didn't have and, as well as offering me my dream job, the police force had great benefits and a good pension. The adverts and everything I read about the force convinced me that it would be the family unit I wanted: once you were in, they looked after you. The camaraderie and teamwork appealed and, at the crux of it, I'd get to help people, something I liked the thought of doing.

I was twenty-one when I applied to join the force. I'd attended an open day to attract new recruits. They had firearms officers, dog handlers, the drug squad and special operations. The choices were vast, but I was set on the dog-handling unit. It's not a role you walk straight into, though. When you complete your sixteen-week training, you're on probation for two years as a bobby on the beat before you can apply for any jobs that become available in the different branches of the force.

In June 2002, I was accepted onto the training programme for Greater Manchester Police and it was one of the best days of my life. I called Mum and Dad instantly when I got the letter and they were delighted for me. Mum knew it was a childhood dream realised and, while she's never been one for effusive praise, she told me I'd done a good job and that she was proud of me. Dad was bristling with pride too; I'd made good on my word and worked hard to get there. They'd always worried about me because I didn't access the same education my siblings did, so for them my job offer into the police was proof the risk had paid off, that I'd succeeded despite not wanting the same opportunities as my brothers and sister. By then Suzanne was at medical school and Gavin was sixteen and starting college, doing A-levels he hoped would give him the grades to get to law school.

I told Denver the good news too and because he was a dog he shared my excitement, his tail wagging but clearly unsure of what we were celebrating.

The four-month training would start at Sedgley Park, Greater Manchester, a huge, sprawling purpose-built centre that saw thousands of recruits pass out every year. Training then moved to Bruche in Warrington. The site is now closed but tens of thousands of officers from fifteen constabularies across the UK all trained there. It was the centre of the majority of UK police training in the sixty years it was open before closure in 2007, a few years after I'd passed through there.

The night before the course started, I spent the entire evening getting everything sorted. I polished my shoes to within an inch of their lives, pressed my suit and shirt three times over to make sure everything was perfect and neatly laid out everything I'd need. This was the first day of the rest of my life and I was determined to make a good impression.

I had an early night and, despite not much sleep because I was too excited, when my alarm went off the next morning I sprang out of bed like a kid at Christmas. Walking downstairs to get my suit before I showered, a smell I wasn't familiar with started wafting up the stairs and a sheepish-looking Denver refused to hold my gaze: he'd puked up all over my suit and shoes. I could have cried. I didn't have any spares as I hardly ever wore a suit, only for weddings, and so I didn't have a plan B.

An hour later, after I'd intended to make a good impression among the trainers and the other 399 new recruits, I rocked up in trainers, a jumper and jeans slightly smelling of the dog sick I'd spent an hour trying to clean off the floor. I could tell my wardrobe hadn't gone unnoticed despite no one saying anything out loud until lunchtime.

The officer in charge gave a series of introductions to the training staff and told us a brief history of Sedgley Park – it was where Moors murderer Myra Hindley stayed when she was taken up onto Saddleworth Moor to identify the graves. Steeped in history, it was the place where we'd go from civilians to serving police officers.

There was a quiet hum while everyone ate lunch until my name was called. I stood where I was and the training inspector who'd done the introductions dressed me down in front of all the other recruits because of my wardrobe choices. I tried to explain but was greeted with the truth that part of being a police officer is learning to adapt. The training officer was right and all I could do was take his criticisms while silently cursing the mongrel who'd caused them.

While my clothes most definitely put me on the training staff's radar, I didn't do anything to help myself after lunch. All new recruits were put in a huge horseshoe shape and the inspector in charge of training went round us all one by one asking what branch we wanted to specialise in. I was the only one who said dog handler and, at this, he burst out laughing.

'That's dead man's shoes, that is, lad! Good luck with that. Is there anything else you want to do?'

'No, I want to be a handler,' I insisted.

We crossed paths a few years later after I'd started as a handler and I asked him to explain what he'd meant that day.

'Once you're on the Dog Unit, you'll never want to give it up.'

He was right: it's the best job in the world.

If you think about the most exciting thing you've ever done and times it by ten, then think about doing it every day with your best friend and getting paid for it, that's what being a police dog handler is like. It's the best game of hide and seek ever. Every dog owner knows how much fun it is to play with your dog. I knew if I worked hard and passed out with flying colours, I'd be able to play with my dog every single day and get paid for it. Yes, there's a cost and a risk to chasing baddies but, ultimately, to your dog it's a game.

I didn't know it when I was training but when the general public get in trouble, they phone the police, and when the police get in trouble, they phone the dog handlers. Turning up to a scene and getting your dog out the van calms everyone. It's like the cavalry have arrived. Us dog handlers have experience of so many different types of crimes because we're called to everything and with that experience comes an air of calm. It's partly because the dogs are so protective of us too and they know how to solve violence fast. One good dog is better than ten people on the ground. Faced with the prospect of a police officer unleashing their dog, a lot of villains decide to come quietly rather than keep on fighting.

I remember once turning up to a job and a massive fight was kicking off. Backup was on the way, but there were a few patrol cars there. The police were backing off and a handler with more experience than me had got out of his van with his dog and asked: 'Who rules these streets? Who's in charge of the streets? It's the police! Now, let's go and sort this job out.' He wasn't violent – he didn't need to unleash his dog because he had experience and just having his dog beside him made everyone who was fighting think twice about continuing.

As he got his dog back in the van afterwards, he told me the best bit of kit any police officer has is their mouth. Sitting in the training school, being laughed at for saying I wanted to be a dog handler, I didn't know any of that, but I was determined to get the job I'd wanted since childhood and nothing was going to put me off it.

2

OUT OF 400 RECRUITS on that first day, I was the only one who wanted to work on the Dog Unit. There were 136 handlers in Greater Manchester Police in 2002 and I was determined to be one of them.

I passed out at the end of September that year and started my two years' probationary policing. You see all sorts when you're newly qualified and the experience you gain means by the time you come to apply for a speciality, you have become a developed all-round officer with street experience.

As well as dogs, I loved fast cars and when a job came out of division – where all the vacancies ended up – in the undercover car branch, I applied. I was told my application was impressive but there were more experienced officers applying. However, I was offered a six-month secondment into the branch when I heard about two spots that had come up on the Dog Division. I was desperate to get one of these jobs and turned down the secondment, putting all my eggs in one basket.

My excitement at getting to apply for my dream job was soon tempered, though. Denver hadn't been himself for a while and the same day I heard about the jobs coming up, I had a call from the vet. Tests done the day before had revealed Denver had bladder cancer and it was advanced. He went downhill fast and I had to have him put to sleep just weeks after the initial diagnosis. It was the biggest shock of my life to that point. I was devastated and it took me years to get over my loss.

Despite treatment and pain relief, Denver's quality of life massively deteriorated in the weeks following the initial diagnosis. He went from jumping up to greet me when I came home from work to limping towards me in pain. I was still taking him out, but where once he'd enjoyed walks for miles and miles, even a few times round the block left him exhausted. He'd always been so alert, ears pricked and ready for something exciting to happen, and suddenly seemed tired all the time. It was like he was ebbing away before my very eyes. He'd rapidly become a shadow of the dog he once was and I knew it wasn't fair to keep him going. Selfishly, I wanted to keep him alive because I loved him and couldn't contemplate life without him but I knew I had to do what was right by him in the same way he'd always done what was right by me.

On advice from the vet and using my intuition, I made the appointment to have Denver put to sleep just five weeks after he was diagnosed. I talked to him and explained what would happen. Of course he didn't understand me but his tired eyes looked into mine for the longest time before I let him up in my bed for the final night's sleep of his life.

The ten-minute drive to the vet the following morning was awful. I wanted every light to stay on red forever so I could keep him with me, but each time they turned green we inched closer to a world without Denver in it.

The vet said I didn't have to be present but there was no way I'd let my dog draw his last breath looking into the eyes of a stranger. Watching him go, seeing him draw his last breath, is forever etched inside me. He was part of me. I loved him and I was never the same after he died.

Denver didn't ask for anything, he just gave and gave and gave. He gave me so much love, he made me laugh, he listened to me rant on about work or friends or family. He did his best with all the training we did, he was loyal and he loved me just as much as I loved him. But then when he went, Denver took all that love with him. I was so angry when he died, it's hard to describe but I'll always be angry with Denver for dying.

As Denver grew progressively sicker, my application for the Dog Unit was going through the appropriate channels. A friend I had at division – Phil, who had finished his probation before me – was applying too and I'd heard through the grapevine there were fifteen applicants across the division for the two positions.

After weeks of waiting, my interview time came up. It was with the Head of the Dog Unit and the Divisional Commander. The first question loomed large but I was expecting it: 'Why should I interview you as a dog handler?'

'I've got a vocation for dogs. I love dogs, I've had dogs throughout my life, and I get them and they get me. I know that means nothing, I've got no experience of what police dogs are, but I want this job and it's one I've wanted since I was a nipper.'

'Correct. That's what I wanted to hear!' was the reply I got.

The rest of the interview went well. I showed I had experience, I had a good track record for arrests and had behaved impeccably during my time on probation. Desperate for a 'yes', I knew that I wouldn't find out for a week.

I was in the nick at the end of a shift when I heard. It was before the time of emails and the chief inspector called and gave me the news which would change my life forever. He said I was young in service but they were really impressed with how I'd progressed. I'd start at the kennels in Hough End, Manchester, the following week for a thirteen-week training programme. I'd be given my own dog and would learn how to search, track and detain. It was a dream come true and by the time I hung up the phone I was buzzing and couldn't contain my excitement. If I said thank you once during the conversation, I must have said it twenty times. I was in shock when we hung up, stunned I'd managed to land the job of my dreams on the first go.

I was still struggling with the loss of Denver. I'd had him cremated and his ashes were on the mantelpiece at home. I felt bereft without him and hated putting my key in the door because, every time I did, the absence of his wagging tail and nuzzling head on the other side felt unbearable but this was a ray of light. Not only was I getting my dream job, I'd have a dog back in the house again.

It was a very small pay rise, but a pay rise nonetheless. I'd get an extra £5 a day in my wage to compensate for the extra work I'd be doing outside of shifts, walking a dog, grooming and generally taking care of them. I was buzzing, absolutely beaming from ear to ear. I called Mum and Dad, who were over the moon. I was twenty-five and I had my dream job. Then I rang my sister Suzanne and my brother Gavin too, who were both delighted for me.

The dog course is at the Greater Manchester Police training kennels in Hough End, near Stockport. There's a smell about it; the first thing you notice is the pungency – a mixture of wet dog and haylage (fermented forage) because the GMP horses are stabled up there as well. It's an unmistakable smell, one you'll never forget the second it hits your nostrils for the first time, but a really welcoming one too. When I turn up there every shift, there's something about breathing in that scent deeply when I get out of my car that makes me feel like I'm home, a part of me is back where it belongs.

For all the welcoming nature of the scent, though, it's a daunting place. There's a hierarchy among handlers and when you're a new recruit, you're no one. Within minutes of starting on day one, I went from thinking I had my dream job to wondering if I'd made the right decision. I was an accomplished police officer in my twenties but now I instantly felt like a little lad on his first day at school.

I asked a handler who was coming out of his van where I should go.

'Why the hell should I tell you?' was his response as he walked away from me and through a door I'd follow.

I found my way to the canteen and saw a familiar face. The friend I had who'd applied at the same time – Phil – had secured the other position on the team. I'd never been so pleased to see anyone in my life. We said our hellos just as a mountain of a man came strolling through the door to greet us.

Dave Johnson was from Wigan and he had hands like shovels. He was huge and had an air of authority about him that I still wouldn't mess with to this day. He explained we'd be working long hours, that training would be split up into different skills, but the dogs were the priority, and at the start and end of each and every day we'd be expected to muck them out and get them sorted. It would mean an extra hour or two on top of our normal working day but the Dog Unit wasn't for the faint-hearted. Like many branches of the police, the training would be tough to root out the ones who had the mettle for it and those who didn't.

After our warm welcome from Dave we were taken to the kennels for the moment I'd been waiting for: we were being allocated our dogs, the partners we'd serve with for years to come. I was still feeling anxious but my nerves gave way to excitement as soon as we approached the kennel block.

It's worth pointing out here that being given your dog is a rite of passage for every handler but what often happens – which new recruits don't know – is that the pairing doesn't always work the first time around. While I was desperate for one of the fourteen-week-old German Shepherd puppies we were walking by, Dave stopped outside a kennel that had an aggressive-looking German Shepherd in it by the name of Simba – he was four and huge. I'd find out later they'd purposefully given me Simba because he was the biggest dog they had and I was only 5ft 7in.

Standing in front of his kennel with some bars separating us, Simba was snarling and growling with his top lip curled up. I'd never seen anything like it.

'There's your dog, G, go and get him.'

(G became my nickname on joining the police force and it's still with me to this day. Gareth when I'm not in uniform, G when I am.)

Dave handed me a lead and gestured for me to open the kennel.

Clearing my throat, I squared my shoulders and unlatched the door. Somehow I managed to get in and get his lead on but the second I brought him out of the kennel, Simba nearly yanked my arm off and I almost ended up on the deck.

It was horrible. Everyone was watching, everyone was there; it's something that stays with you forever the first time you get your dog out. I'd dreamt of the moment so many times, it's all I'd wanted for decades, but rather than be the magical moment I'd always longed for, it was one of the only moments I've ever wanted the earth to open up and swallow me. Even thinking about it now I get goosebumps and feel a bit sick about how badly it went.

I could have cried as I handed Dave the lead and walked out without a backwards glance. Afterwards I gave myself an internal pep talk: 'Come on, Gareth, this is what you've always wanted. You've dreamed of this job for years and you're going to give it up the first hour you've started just because some dog has pulled you? You've come all this way, don't moan, get on with it!'

With that began my thirteen weeks of hell.

Day two started with a lecture from Dave Johnson, the crux of which was that whatever you're feeling as a handler will go down the lead and into your dog. Dogs are such intuitive creatures and have worked alongside humans for thousands of years, our bond being the strongest of any two species on the planet, but with that bond comes a responsibility. If a handler is stressed taking a dog into an already stressful situation like a fight, there's a risk that things could go wrong and the dog could act of its own accord. If you are calm and focused, your dog will be that way too. But if you are erratic, panicked, over-zealous or angry, your dog will be the same. It's vital you behave in exactly the same way as you want your dog to behave.

We'd start with simple commands, sit and heel and recall work, and move onto the more complex matters like biting as the course progressed. It was such an emotional roller coaster, Dave's advice on day one was hard to stick to sometimes. Simba was never pleased to see me but we tolerated each other. Four years old, he had been given to the unit by his owners, who couldn't handle him anymore. He had natural aggression, he was a tough dog and he was brand new to the unit, which was the only thing we had in common. We didn't bond straight away and he liked to play me. One day he'd sit and do exactly as I told him, the next he'd ignore every command, leaving me frustrated and looking like I didn't know what I was doing. I'd go from the high of controlling a huge Shepherd to the frustration of being treated like a fool by something with four legs.

I soon learned that timing is massive when it comes to praising your dog and that you have a small window to reinforce positive behaviours and get rid of negative ones. Get it wrong with the moment you praise or admonish them and you can mess them up completely. If you're struggling with recall and screaming at your dog to come back and he does and you shout at him, he'll associate coming back with being shouted at.

When you're teaching him to sit, even when his bum hits the floor for a split second, you need to notice the second itself and praise him. As a new recruit all I'd hear for ages was 'You've missed your chance, you should have praised them then.' Timing has now become second nature to me, like it was for all the trainers who taught me, but it takes some time to learn to get it right.

Life at Hough End wasn't for the faint-hearted. The daily routine started at six o'clock every morning:

Go to your kennel, get your dog out
Put him in the wagon, come back
Muck the kennel out, go back to the wagon
Get your dog, groom him
Go to the canteen to make tea and toast for all the
    trainers (it had to be Lurpak butter, anything else
    just wouldn't do and you'd get berated before

31

being sent back to the shop to get the proper
stuff)
Start the day's training after tea and toast

Every day was Groundhog Day. It was September,
absolutely Baltic and it rained every single day. You'd
finish at 3 o'clock, only you didn't finish because
you'd have to sort your dog out. It was Monday to
Friday but you'd be expected to go to the kennels on
Saturdays and Sundays and do the same routine of
taking care of your dog before using your initiative and
training them on things they'd been weaker on during
the week.

As well as the act of training the dogs and preparing
them for a life of front-line policing, the whole training
programme was designed to test you to see how badly
you wanted the job. The training got tougher as the
weather got colder. Everyone's hands were in ribbons.
We were working with long lines that would zip through
your hands and leave them dry and cracked, but on day
one Dave had decreed anyone who came with plasters
would be off the course: 'No one's going to come and
help you at 2 a.m. when it's lashing wind and freezing
rain and you're on a track in a forest in the middle of
nowhere that's just dried up. You have to be able to help

yourself and get used to working in uncomfortable conditions.' I needed to be toughened up and while Dave's way of doing it might not have been to everyone's taste, it worked for me.

Phil, the pal who had got the other job on the Dog Unit when I got mine, severed his index finger one day a few weeks into the course. He was bitten by the dog he was training and had to go to A&E. They patched him up and told him to rest his finger, but the next day Dave had him straight on tracking.

You hold the lead loosely in your hand and rest it over your index finger when tracking so the dog can head off and use the length of the lead if they need to but so you've got a hold on them to keep them safe and out of harm's way. If a tracking dog comes to a main road, they'll get themselves run over by their singular dedication to follow a track.

They started us on tracking that day just because Phil had hurt himself and it would test his mettle to hold the long line like that for the whole day against his injured finger. There was no other reason for it. Everything was about making a point and testing how much you wanted it. Phil still can't straighten his finger properly as a result of that day but not for one second did he think about complaining or quitting.

Six weeks into the course, while Simba had become more pliable and we'd accepted each other as partners, I was struggling to get him to lie down. I was so frustrated by it but, remembering what Dave had said about my feelings going down the lead, I tried staying patient. As he'd done on day one too, Simba still strained at the lead and pulled when I got him out, something I'd have to get a handle on before we could pass out.

It was a dark and cold December afternoon when Dave decided he'd had enough of watching me struggle.

'Check him back.'

Dave wanted me to issue Simba with a command that would bring him back to my side – a tug on his lead should have done it. I checked him to heel and looped the length of the long lead underneath my arm. Clearly dissatisfied with how I'd done it, Dave let out a long sigh and marched over to me. He stood between Simba and me, and using his 17-stone weight compared to my 9½-stone weight he pulled Simba back. Simba wasn't used to such force, though, and turned around. As I was standing in between Dave and Simba, he latched onto me and rather than go for one bite, he bit me on the arm five or six times before I managed to get him under control. Dave watched the whole thing unfold before uttering, 'That was your fault, lad,' and walking off.

A fellow trainer on the course could see I was in pain, angry, upset and ready to answer back. 'Eyes open, ears open, gob shut,' he said before following Dave back towards the canteen.

Convinced I'd lost my job on the unit, I walked Simba back to the wagon. He bit me again before I could get him in the wagon and I knew, even if my time on the unit wasn't over, I couldn't work Simba, he'd lost any respect for me that I'd worked hard at gaining.

Every day on the unit ended with a brief appraisal and, more than any other day, I was dreading mine. Simba had broken the skin on my arm and I was in agony but sat dutifully and waited for Dave to begin.

'How do you think today went then, lad?'

'It could have been better ...' I trailed off, exhausted, in pain, cold, tired and upset.

'Yep, you're right there. See you tomorrow.'

That night was agony. You don't stitch a dog bite unless it's very serious because their mouths are germ-laden and you need to make sure you wash out your wound. I was in pain and worried sick about what the next day would yield.

Walking in to Simba the next day it was like he'd forgotten yesterday had happened. He let me lead him out to the wagon without any fuss at all and I started to think maybe my luck had changed. After all, I'd been bitten. I'd taken it like a real dog handler; maybe it was the initiation I needed and everything would be fine. I dared to start feeling a little sunnier about the whole thing but that changed the second I presented Dave with his morning tea and toast.

'Take your dog out the van, you're not having him anymore. That's you done!' I was told.

Somehow I managed to get out into the open air before tears started streaming down my cheeks. My dream job, the one I'd wanted since I was a lad, was done. I was out, it was over. I felt humiliated, hurt and angry, but above all else I was bereft. I didn't have a plan B and my plan A had been ripped from me for something I felt wasn't my fault. But I did as I was told and pulled myself together before I got back in front of Dave.

'We don't know what we're going to do with you – possibly send you back to division and we don't think you're going to come back, so we'll see …'

It was brutal. I'd rather they took me into the yard and beat me up. Physical pain I'd learned to deal with, but this was an emotional pain and I was hurting at the thought of getting so close to my dream only to have it potentially snatched away from me.

3

WHILE I SPENT THE REST of the day feeling sorry for myself, unsure of what my future held, but knowing better than to ask or make a fuss, I was able to observe things way more than I had when I'd been busy with Simba. I could see there were high-level discussions going on between Dave and a man called Paul Quinlan, who was a trainer in charge of the breeding programme for Greater Manchester Police.

As I sat trying not to be noticed, drinking my now-cold tea, I could see Paul shaking his head and telling Dave 'no' in no uncertain terms. At the time I had no idea what the discussions entailed, but I later learned Dave was telling Paul he needed an extra dog. The dogs Paul was working with were supposed to go to experienced handlers only. Police dogs can only work until they're around eight or eight and a half before they're retired, usually to the handler who has run them during their career. Puppies mostly go to those with experience who are on their second or third dog. Their argument was getting heated but I knew better than to presume the dog would be for me. Another officer on the course didn't have a dog because he hadn't gelled with any he'd been given so I presumed the new dog – if it came off – was for him.

Paul reluctantly finally agreed. Dave was a man used to getting his way and later that day I saw Riley for the first time. A ten-month-old German Shepherd, something about him immediately captured me. He had a brindle stripe (sometimes called 'tiger striping', the term is used to describe a dog's coat where the stripes or patches are almost the same colour as the base coat) and was absolutely beautiful. Indeed, Riley was a Ferrari compared to Simba, who had been like a Ford Fiesta. He went straight to the officer who didn't have a dog as I had expected and I spent a week on the course without a dog.

If it had been hard before, it was even harder without a dog to train. I did all the chores, got everyone their tea and coffee and toast, mucked out, brushed and got all the dogs their food and water. I was a lackey but knew better than to utter anything about my future or what would happen. Every time I'd pass Dave he'd tell me he had yet to hear from division about what would happen to me. With hindsight, I know now that it was all a test: they were seeing how resilient I was, how much I could cope with and how much I could take. The thing about dog handling is you can't lose your rag, you can't get stressed and upset or start shouting the odds. You need to be even-tempered and have a quiet, stealthy resilience. Dave was pushing me all the time to see if I'd throw the towel in or have a go at him about the unfairness of the circumstances because I was idling and growing bored, but I didn't. I don't think they had any intention of putting me off the dogs, they were just testing me to see how much I could take.

The officer who was with Riley was struggling with him. They hadn't gelled and Dave called me to one side while we were training in the woods one day.

'If you could have any dog on this course and it might mean someone getting kicked off the course, could you do it?'

'Yeah, I can do that.'

'Even your friends?'

'Yep.'

'Right, what dog would you take if you could have it now?'

As little experience as I had, I wasn't stupid: I asked for Riley straight away.

'What about Max?' came the reply.

Now Max was a horrible dog. He was huge, bigger than Simba, and I knew he'd be a successful police dog because he had a natural aggression but he wasn't a dog I wanted or relished the thought of handling. I didn't trust his temperament and, though I was new to the unit, my gut instinct told me no one would be able to handle him and, ultimately, he'd come off the dog section.

'Look, if you're telling me I've got to have Max, I'll have him,' I said, resigned to getting whatever dog they decreed I'd have, but just as I was about to let out a huge sigh, the words I wanted to hear came out …

'Okay,' he said, 'you can have Riley.'

The officer who'd had Riley was sent back to division and I was given Riley. It was week seven of the thirteen-week course. I had some catching up to do if he was going to pass out in just six weeks.

Those six weeks were amazing! I went from wondering about my future on the unit to knowing I was exactly where I was meant to be. The daily appraisals almost always talked about how I was a natural with dogs. Riley learned fast, listened well and had a natural aptitude for training. One of the finest-bred dogs I've ever worked with, he was like a sponge – he got everything I taught him and never forgot anything in between sessions. We caught up with the other recruits within a fortnight. Riley passed out with flying colours and I learned I'd be sent back to the division I'd come from as their dog handler.

It was the proudest day of my life, and Riley and I started spending our entire lives together. Us recruits knew when we were training that we'd spend our first six weeks as handlers paired with another dog handler and their dog. It's one thing learning it all at Hough End, another thing altogether to put it into practice on the street.

The dog-handling partner I was paired with was Andy Beaver, who had been a tutor while I'd been training. He was a great guy and, while I wanted Riley and I to go straight into the fray, I knew there were worse handlers I could have been paired with as we bedded ourselves in. Andy's dog was called Milo, a German Shepherd. They'd worked together for around a year and Milo was an excellent police dog. Now retired, Andy's one of my best friends and in those six weeks he taught me so much. He showed me what confidence can do and how teamwork between you and a dog should go.

Milo was big and daft, but he was fantastic when he needed to be. We'd run the dogs together on the field during the shift, but nine times out of ten Milo would disappear off chasing a rabbit, something he would never have dreamt of doing on an actual job or a rural track. He had a great recall but would forget you'd called him back and would disappear again to chase something else; he was dippy but with a beautiful temperament.

Andy showed me what a relationship between a dog and their handler can be like. He'd have thrown himself in front of a car for Milo and Milo would have done the same thing for him. They were a unit and adored each other. I'd watch their body language on searches, becoming one, and ached to have their experience. I wanted Riley and I to be as good or better than they were. It was an amazing six weeks of learning on the job with what turned out to be a lifelong friend.

The first day of our first shift in December 2002, Riley made his first bite. We'd been on shift all night and were called to an estate in Oldham at 1 a.m. I had Riley on a long line and as we searched the back of the property, we found a male trying to break into the house. He saw us and started to run off. I used the challenges we'd been taught in training, and when he ignored them I sent Riley in. He bit and detained the man like he should have done but Riley bit his bum, not his arm as he'd been trained to. Two nights later, we caught the same man again doing the same thing and Riley detained him again, this time on his arm.

Looking back, it was a nothing bite and a nothing sort of job: he didn't wound the man or put him in hospital or anything like that, but I felt like I'd arrived – I could say I'd had a bite. I was a new recruit who was earning my place on the team. Over the next couple of years, Riley and I went from strength to strength. A formidable police dog, his success tally kept climbing. He was a fantastic tracker in urban and rural environments, fearless with an amazing bite, and would follow my command to the letter. He was so strong too – nothing got away from him and he knew it.

In October 2005, Riley saved my life for the first time. I didn't think I could have loved him any more than I already did, but it's a job that will stay with me forever. We were at the start of our shift when we were called to someone breaking into an empty derelict pub in Ashton-under-Lyne. We rocked up and were told by officers on the scene that one or two people had gone in and not come out. The officers asked if I wanted them to come in with me but I knew I'd be better with Riley alone so we went in and issued our challenges.

Challenges give perpetrators the time to give themselves up without me sending Riley in or them potentially coming to any harm. Before you release a police dog, you should let people know you're there, so first you call 'Police officer with a dog, come out or I will send in the dog!' If they don't respond, you issue a further challenge of 'Come out now or I'll send in the dog, it's your last warning!' and if they still don't respond, you send in the dog.

I issued the challenges and, as expected, no one gave themselves up. Riley started searching upstairs and cleared the top and ground floor, room by room. After searching for the better part of fifteen minutes in the pitch-black, he eventually took me into the basement. We were barely at the foot of the stairs down when he started to growl so I knew someone was there. I opened a door inwards and Riley shot into the corner. There was a trolley used to carry drinks and a lad was hiding behind it. I lit him up with the torch and told him, 'Stay there, don't move!' The words were barely out of my mouth when Riley spun on me and just came hurtling towards me, baring his teeth. He'd never done anything like it before and for a split second I was confused. In the same split second, out of the corner of my eye, I caught the glint of a crowbar coming down towards my head just as Riley caught the arm holding the crowbar in mid-air. I didn't issue any command for him to do that; I hadn't trained him to look after me, I'd trained him to catch criminals. Riley had taken the initiative himself.

Our bond meant he'd wanted to protect me.

While the two men were arrested, I took Riley back to the van and gave him a drink and a fuss. I thanked him and remembered one of the things Dave Johnson had taught us recruits while we were training as handlers. I didn't get what he was talking about at the time but he'd told us, 'If you look after these dogs properly for twelve months, they will look after you for the rest of their lives.' From that moment, I swore I'd never let anything happen to Riley. If that crowbar had hit me, I could have died instantly. He'd saved my life and I was indebted to him.

By the start of 2006, I grew to rely on Riley; he became my rock and we became part of each other. There's a saying in the Dog Unit that you can call me what you like, call me everything under the sun, but you call my dog anything or tell it to shut up and you see how a handler will react.

As Riley developed into a confident police dog, I became a confident handler, but where dogs aren't prone to arrogance, the same cannot be said for humans. Riley was a fantastic piece of kit, an amazing partner and a wonderful dog. We were fast becoming a successful team and I'd park 'Gareth' at the gates of every shift and become 'G'.

Gareth is a bit of a sap who wears his heart on his sleeve but I had to present a tougher exterior at work, bordering on arrogance and cockiness. Dealing with criminals who've taken something that doesn't belong to them or hurt someone who was minding their own business can be emotionally draining so I'd switch persona at the start of each shift as much for self-preservation as anything else. There were times that winter when we'd be on tracks in fields, on the moors or in the woods in the middle of nowhere. It'd be dark, we'd be lost and looking for someone with a knife or a gun, but G felt invincible with Riley beside him.

It was while feeling invincible that I met Claire in January 2007. She was a police community support officer at the time and the PCSO team worked out of Hyde nick, where Riley and I were stationed. I saw a picture of her before I met her in the flesh and was blown away by how stunning she was. I'd finished a job and was doing the paperwork and needed a pen so I wandered over to an empty desk to grab one, not knowing it was hers. There was a framed picture of a woman with blonde hair and a lad sitting on her lap. I was struck by Claire but equally drawn to the fact she loved her son enough to have a picture up on her desk of the two of them. Her hands were round his waist and I couldn't see a wedding ring. A quick enquiry of the officer on the desk next to hers confirmed she was single. I wasn't looking for anyone – I was busy with work and Riley was my life, both in and out of the nick, but I couldn't get her out of my head.

When I met her in person a few days later, I had no idea how much she'd change my life. Riley and I had been on a massive track which resulted in nothing. We got back to the station after three hours in the middle of Saddleworth Moor. I was freezing cold and shouted for someone to make me a brew. Claire popped her head round the door and asked, 'Are you tired, Gareth?'

I remember thinking, *Oh my God, she knows my name! Oh my God!*

She made me a brew and we had a bit of small talk, but her shift was ending and she had to pick her son Ben up. Instantly infatuated, I didn't have the courage to ask her out because I was scared she'd say no. Over the course of the next few weeks, though, our paths would cross and, while we'd always chat, it never went any further. Her dad had been a dog handler in the police for twenty-six years and she was a natural with Riley. He adored her and she'd give him treats she kept in her desk. Before too long, both of us got excited every time we saw her.

I'd stay behind at work just to see her come on shift. I wouldn't talk to her as she'd be busy with the hand-over, but just seeing her made me happy. I liked watching the way she'd scrape her hair back and get it smart and out of the way before she started and how she'd bite the top of her pen while taking notes. I could have watched her forever, it was like she had some kind of magnetism over me. Just being near her made me feel better about everything.

One day in February 2007, it had been lashing down with rain and I'd been on patrol with Riley. He was in the wagon and I popped into the station before we headed off on another job. Claire was on her way out and I asked what she was doing that day. She was on her way to a patrol around the town but I knew she'd get soaking wet because of the weather. I gave her my mobile number and told her to message me if she needed a lift back to the station to keep her dry.

My phone lit into life an hour later: 'I hope you're okay and not too wet, I've got some treats for the worker and that's not you, that's for Riley.'

I texted her back, saying, 'How dare you abuse my phone in this manner! It's for professional work purposes only.'

She didn't skip a beat before she replied: 'Have you got anything else I can abuse ...?'

Our relationship was born.

We were both very cocky and very confident. The spark between us was undeniable and things moved quickly. Claire was very upfront about Ben from the second we got together. She explained they came as a package: 'So if you don't accept him, you don't get me.'

I loved how upfront and forthright she was. I'd been as drawn to Ben as I was to Claire, and within a few weeks of our first date I met him for the very first time. He was four and a gorgeous little lad; he was sitting on my knee in a few minutes and taking cookies from the jar. Riley adored both Claire and Ben and we moved in together a couple of months after we met. I'd gone from being a single bloke with a career my life revolved around to someone who was coupled up, with a little lad in the house. It was perfect and my readymade family was all I could have wished for. I'd been saving hard since starting on the job unit and was in the process of completing on a house when I met Claire so it made sense for her and Ben to move in with me rather than for us to find somewhere else.

My family were delighted I'd found Claire too. Work had been really intense for months and, all of a sudden, I had a balance I didn't know I'd been missing. Meanwhile, Riley and I were going from one amazing job to another. Fellow handlers would tell me we were making a name for ourselves. I remember one saying, 'The criminals are in bed at 10 o'clock when they know you're on duty.'

We had a job in April 2008, a 'missing from home' – someone had disappeared and we were tasked with seeing if Riley could get the scent and try and find him or her. It was a horrendous night. There was so much rain the rivers had flooded and a raging torrent. Riley was a strong swimmer but fell in and I knew he was panicking. I didn't think twice about following him in, but shouted I'd need someone downstream fast to help us both get out. The last thing I heard before I hit the icy torrent was the divisional inspector on the radio shouting, 'Do not go in that river!'

Hitting the water took my breath away. When I surfaced, Riley was just a few feet away and I was able to grab him by the scruff of the neck. I got us both onto the bank, breathless, cold and wet. Riley went berserk, licking my face, shaking the water off and then licking and nuzzling me more. 'You silly bugger!' I laughed, even though I was starting to shiver. 'Don't do that again, you could have drowned and so could I.'

In 2008, Riley and I were unstoppable. We worked hard, knew each other inside out and our success rate was huge. Ben and Claire were perfect at home and while 'G' had become a force to be reckoned with, the last thing he needed was an even more inflated ego, then *Send in the Dogs* happened. An ITV documentary following police handlers, it ran for two seasons and covered dog handlers in forces including Nottingham, London, Yorkshire and Manchester, which is where I came in.

4

BY THE START OF 2009, Riley was Greater Manchester Police's stud dog, which meant he sired 58 puppies. We'd also made it to three National Police Dog Trials Championships, where the best police dogs across all the forces in the UK compete. I wasn't able to go, but the fact he'd qualified was a huge thing for me, a testament to the work we'd been putting in together and how successful we were becoming. As well as flying at work, Claire, Ben and I were becoming a real little unit.

There'd been rumours at work for a while that we were going to be one of the forces on the second series of the ITV show *Send in the Dogs*. I was desperate to be a part of it, but wouldn't have said so out loud. While Riley and I were a very successful team and had a great arrest record between us, we weren't exactly a modest pairing. It's embarrassing to admit now, but I even had a hoodie I wore to work that I had specially printed. It said: 'If you run, you'll only go to jail with teeth marks.'

Looking back, I was an idiot. A complete idiot.

With the power of hindsight, I'm pretty sure the powers that be decided my already inflated ego didn't need a primetime TV show. I was gutted – I knew the jobs Riley and I went on would make some great TV but I also knew I'd rubbed people who made the decisions up the wrong way so I wasn't surprised when I wasn't chosen. I pretended I wasn't bothered at all but I'd have given anything to be involved.

I started 2009 with a small chip on my shoulder but it grew as the months went on. I didn't expect to be praised for every job, but Riley and I had a fantastic arrest record. I'd go on call-outs that would take hours, minutes before my shift finished, while other handlers didn't, and I started to resent how hard I was working compared to some other handlers I knew. I should have just kept my head down and ploughed on, but I was becoming obnoxious and thought someone above me should have sorted it out. I'm taking full responsibility for the idiot I was becoming, but when you're doing well and you're bringing in great results, it's hard not to believe the hype and start to think you're the best at what you do.

I was still a comparatively novice handler – yes, I was gaining experience and knew what I was doing more every day, every job – but Claire had twenty-six years' experience of being around a dog handler. Her dad had been one of the most successful of his generation so she could see I wasn't behaving as he'd done.

Send in the Dogs was still being filmed at work and there was a cameraman – Paddy – who everyone in the unit got on with. He'd been out with a few handlers and got plenty of different material, but I knew he and the team wanted a bite on camera. It was the one thing they hadn't had so far in the months of filming they'd done. Paddy loved a brew and spent a lot of time in the canteen, which is how he got to know the handlers he wasn't shadowing as well as the ones he was. He was eating lunch one day when I overheard him saying how good it would be to get the first televised bite in UK TV history, there had never been one caught on camera before. Before I could stop myself, my ego piped up, 'It's because you're following the wrong people. If you come with me, I'll give you exactly what you want.'

Of course, I couldn't promise that, let alone deliver, but I managed to convince Paddy, who spoke to his superiors. The handler he'd been following was scheduled for a week of annual leave anyway so it all timed out perfectly. I was finally on the *Send in the Dogs* rota of handlers and, while my superiors can't have been especially chuffed about it, I was delighted and, true to my word in the week I filmed, I got the first police dog bite on film ever shown in the UK.

Throughout the filming, the Tameside division was getting pillaged with car thefts yet no one had been caught or arrested despite surveillance and a lot of police hours going into finding the gang who were responsible. Part of what makes me a successful police officer is growing up on an estate wracked by crime. From a pretty young age I was exposed to how criminals think so I'd long been able to connect the dots and use intuition to steer my policing.

I had a copper's nose, which develops over time when you're a police officer and any serving or retired officer will know what I mean. Even when you're off-shift, you can't help but notice the car that goes off the main road and through the estate instead of taking a shortcut on the main road. You instantly see when a number plate is newly screwed on; you simply know when to pursue things that don't look as they should and it's something you only learn from experience – it can't be taught at Bruche or Sedgley Park.

Whenever we've had gangs or teams working as a criminal unit on a spree I've always been one who'll spend hours poring over crime scenes and reports. I do all the background work, look at all the crime scene pictures, read all the reports, track all the dates … It's hard to describe because there's alchemy to it. There's no one thing that's teachable but with experience on the job you get to know how criminals think and, once you know, you can go some way towards trying to work out what their next steps could be. It's good old-fashioned police work and I love it.

With Paddy to impress, I spent more time than usual going over every shred of evidence for the gang we had so far. I meticulously studied time frames, locations and photographs, looking for anything that might help figure out who they were and what they might do next. I knew I was on to something and closing in when Paddy announced one Wednesday that he had to go and film another part of Greater Manchester Police. I told him there was a chance he'd miss what he wanted, but he told me it wasn't his decision to make and he'd be back with me the following night. So I dropped him off in the van where he needed to go and was on my way back to the station when the call came across the radio: there was a pursuit happening in Oldham.

There'd been a burglary and the two guys involved had taken a Volvo and a Polo from the driveway of the house. I'd been researching and studying this group and where they went and what they did and, because I felt like I knew them, I went to a route where my copper's nose told me they'd be. I knew they'd taken two cars and, sure enough, I saw them both exactly where I thought they'd be. I had to make a split-second decision to go after one of the cars so I chose the Polo, reckoning my van could keep up with it better than it could a Volvo.

Within a few minutes of the pursuit starting, the car crashed into a wall and the occupant inside set off on foot into a housing estate. Riley and I followed and, while we gave chase, I issued the challenges, which were ignored. I sent Riley in and he detained him with one of the cleanest bites I'd ever seen him make. He bit him with such speed and dexterity, the lad went crashing through a garden gate.

Paddy had missed it: we were finally able to make an arrest which led to us getting the rest of the gang. My already-inflated ego and sense of self-worth hit brand new heights. I joked with Paddy that I'd told him so, but the poor lad had to tell his producers the storyline he'd been filming had no culmination because he'd done as he was told and filmed something else.

Working forty to fifty hours a week, thinking you're God's gift to the Dog Unit, inevitably meant some of the arrogance and competitive streak I assumed for around eight hours every day at work stayed with me when I went home. Claire and I had talked at length about having a baby together and by mid-2009, being what can best be described as an arrogant git about it, I promised her if we had the child I desperately wanted, it'd be a girl and the labour would be quick. I know how that sounds and, yes, I was being an idiot, but everything I touched at work was successful so I'd developed a bit of a hero complex and cavalierly made the promise. Of course, Claire knew better than to believe me but I'd promise it every time we'd have a conversation about adding to our family.

With wisdom and experience it's easy to see the way I was behaving both at work and at home was unsustainable, but I couldn't see that at the time. Yes, I was a great handler and we got results, but I took risks that I shouldn't have done, something that caused tension between Claire and me. Claire knew plenty about the Dog Unit and she knew getting into trouble and arguing with the seniors above you wasn't the way to get on. The Dog Unit is a family. It might sound daft but we're a bit like a pack and when someone is stepping out of line when they shouldn't, it doesn't go unnoticed and it's tough to smooth over. It's easy to develop a bad name for yourself and tough to get rid of that label.

Claire had been furious the night I'd jumped in the river after Riley, partly because she was worried and partly because she knew I'd defied a direct order not to get in the water and she knew that defiance always held consequences. She didn't want me getting into trouble, she wanted me to keep my head down and get on with the job.

In November 2009, Riley and I were on our way in a chase when I was clocked by a speed camera doing 96mph in a 40mph zone. Police cars are able to speed but it was excessively fast and the risk to civilians at that speed far outweighed the benefits of getting the car I was chasing. The car had been involved in an armed robbery but because my driving authority didn't allow me to go that fast, I got into trouble and had the book thrown at me.

When any officer is found doing those types of speeds there's an investigation, which happens to ascertain whether the speed was warranted or not. I was grounded, which meant I couldn't drive the police van while they investigated. It was protocol, but it benched Riley and me and meant I couldn't go on jobs. Frustration grew: I wanted to do this role, I was a dog handler with passion and it was like going to work with your hands tied behind your back. I was putting Riley in kennels every day and working another role in general policing while the investigation reached its conclusion – not something that was going to happen fast just because I was frustrated and wanted it to.

It was while I was benched that I had an argument with the chief inspector. I'd had enough of feeling like I was on probation again doing general policing. I couldn't work with Riley and while I desperately wanted to, I also missed him massively. We'd spent every waking moment together since we passed out and suddenly not having him as my partner felt like I'd taken a huge step back. With the luxury of hindsight, I hadn't taken my foot off the brake since we'd started working together. I'd dealt with a lot of tough jobs and nearly lost my life and my dog on some occasions, but my way of coping had been to keep motoring on and take my mind off the worst jobs by going on still more jobs. But with a regular beat and time to think, things were starting to catch up with me and I wasn't coping.

In the meeting with the chief inspector as part of the investigation, I raised my voice and started shouting, not something I should have done and not something any police officer is advised to do. I was already grounded for speeding and now a member of the public had also put in a complaint against me. Before I'd been grounded, Claire's dad had been very ill and I'd stopped by in the van for a few minutes on a shift in between jobs to drop something off to him and check how he was doing. A neighbour had seen Riley in the van and registered a complaint. They were right: I shouldn't have done it during the time I was on shift, but I didn't care about right and wrong. I saw it as a small infringement against a backdrop of massive success. In short, I thought they should give me a longer leash (excuse the pun) because I was such a successful handler. It didn't occur to me for a second that rules are rules and no one is exempt.

The chief inspector tried to see things from my side, telling me just because I was getting good results it didn't mean I was above the establishment, but I was so stubborn I wasn't interested. I'd started to work autonomously but you can't do that when you're in the police: teamwork is what makes us. I managed to get away with a warning for swearing at him but was told in no uncertain terms I was on my last warning.

As I continued general policing, my stress levels went through the roof while the investigation meandered its way towards a conclusion. I was on shift a few weeks after raising my voice and knew I'd hear in the next few days whether the investigation would wrap up without discipline or whether I'd be punished.

I was at my computer in the office when I heard the familiar sound of an email arrive: I was grounded for six and a half months. I felt hot, sick and I saw red. I pushed the computer off my desk, stormed out and that was that. It was January 2010. I knew I'd fucked up. I was moved off the dogs indefinitely while I was disciplined and investigated for speeding, which could take months. In what felt like a heartbeat I'd gone from being the most successful dog handler in Greater Manchester Police with a girlfriend who adored him to a frustrated general police officer who was struggling to communicate with the woman he loved. Claire had been worried sick about what was happening at work but I'd been selfishly so worried about myself, I didn't have the bandwidth to assuage her fears. Stress had inevitably built up and the dynamic of our loving and affectionate relationship had started to change because of me.

Being benched usually meant you'd be back working soon but being moved off indefinitely and facing a disciplinary and an investigation, even being optimistic I knew I wouldn't get back to the unit anytime soon. I was looking at months rather than weeks. It wasn't something I could contemplate no matter how often Claire gently tried to raise the subject.

I started working an office job – I was in uniform every day but doing paperwork, no policing as I saw it. It was a far cry from the shifts I'd loved. I was doing general policing, events in the city, political party conferences. I'd go on shift sometimes and clear out stationery cupboards. I had nothing to do and I hated it – I'd gone from being a respected handler to someone they didn't really know what to do with. All the while there were baddies on the streets who were getting away with crimes while Riley was stuck in kennels getting bored and I was rearranging paper clips.

I'd drop Riley into kennels at Hough End, go to the city centre or the nick and do my day's pedestrian policing, go back to the kennels and get Riley and go home – it was so frustrating. It wasn't Riley's fault he couldn't work, it was mine. In addition to knowing I'd let myself down, I'd also let him down and every single day I felt guilty for that. He was an amazing piece of kit with the capabilities to make the streets safer and put people away but, because I'd been so stupid, he sat languishing with boredom in a kennel. He was really well looked after but he loved to work and, because of me, he couldn't. Pent-up, he couldn't understand why we weren't out on the streets and I couldn't explain it to him.

There are many fantastic things about the Dog Unit and one of them is that they'll never pair your dog to work with anyone else if you're under investigation, facing disciplinary action or off on long-term sickness. The Armed Forces dogs change handlers like they change socks, and by the time an army dog retires he could have been with upwards of ten handlers as deployment rotations mean there need to be changes, but that doesn't happen in the police. When you pass out with your dog or puppy unless there are extenuating circumstances you're partners until they finish their service. The one thing I could rely on was that they'd never take Riley off me to work with another officer: we were a team and they respected that. In the same way that if Riley was injured, I wouldn't work another dog while he recovered.

For me the hardest part was that I didn't know when the period of me being off the dogs would end. Stressed and angry all the time, I wasn't able to work with my dog and I hated being told I couldn't. I was angry, upset and bored – so bored of not being able to do what I'd trained to do. I kept pushing it with every senior officer I could find to get an answer, but no one would commit me to a time frame. I was desperate to get back on the dogs, get back to Riley, but all I could do was learn patience and wait.

While work was increasingly frustrating, the stress Claire and I had been under had thawed. She knew how bereft I was at being taken off the dogs and she knew I'd learned my lesson. Arrogance and ego had brought me to my knees and I accepted 100 per cent of the blame. It meant the fear and worry she'd had for me lessened because she knew I'd be a different handler when I did get back to work with Riley.

In May 2010, I was at work on yet another shift I wasn't invested in when I opened my lunchbox and a note fell to the floor. It was from Claire: she told me she was ready for us to have a baby. I couldn't have been happier – work might have been something I was tolerating rather than loving at that point, but home was finally perfect. Claire was one of the most beautiful women I'd ever seen. I was so proud when she agreed to go out with me and now she was agreeing to have a child with me. For the first time in months, I had something to smile about.

In June of that year we went away to Turkey and Claire fell pregnant. I was working a political party conference when I received a text message from her: 'You're going to be a dad!' Overwhelmed and with my work life in tatters, it was the light at the end of the tunnel I desperately needed. A few hours later, though, towards the end of my shift, I was called into the superintendent's office. I knew I'd get told off – a substantial slap on the wrist – but the thought of finally getting back to work with Riley was something I'd been dreaming about at night. So I put my number one uniform on and, having polished my shoes the previous night, I wanted them to know I took whatever the punishment was seriously. I wanted them to know I accepted the gravitas of the situation and that it wasn't a minor misdemeanour.

I knew from other handlers I worked with and from chatting at the kennels every day when I dropped Riley off that unit arrests had gone down without me working Riley. Now I couldn't wait to make up for lost time and get back on the streets. I knew I wouldn't be the only one happy to be back too – I couldn't wait to get Riley, take him home, celebrate Claire's pregnancy and my return to work. I was thinking about what takeaway we'd get to celebrate when I was called in to the superintendent's office. Rather than a telling-off and some humble pie, his next words floored me: 'You're off the dogs for good, Gareth.'

I didn't hear anything past those words. My whole world fell apart and I felt the room starting to swim around me.

The job I'd dreamed of as a kid was over.

I'd blown it.

Me.

I'd let myself down but, more than that, I'd let Riley down.

I had no pride left and, while I fought back tears and sniffed my way through the meeting, if I apologised once then I said sorry twenty times. I was like a child begging for one more chance, one more go to put things right.

'G' had messed up and Gareth's world was broken.

I was gently told I couldn't behave like I had, that if they let it go unpunished then it could have serious repercussions and they had no choice but to take me off the dogs. Finally, giving in to tears, I asked my last question of the meeting: 'Am I ever going to be allowed to be a dog handler again?' I was told I could apply for future positions, but I had to go away and reflect on what had happened.

5

I WAS GIVEN THE OPTION to rehome Riley to a force or retire him to me and I made the decision to keep him home with me. Even though he was only five and had a lot left to give as a police dog, I knew I couldn't cope without him. He was part of the family and Claire adored him as much as I did.

I was sent to a neighbourhood office as a PC.

I'd talked for hours with Claire about what happened. I knew I was lucky to still be a serving police officer – I could have been kicked off the force completely, which would have meant not only my childhood dream in tatters, but a father and partner with no way to support his family.

While I'd been taken off the Dog Unit, the one glimmer of hope was that I could reapply if a position came up. It meant being patient, not stepping out of line and making sure I did as good a job as I could until an opening came up.

I've always been a fast learner and, while I was bereft and had taken it hard, I knew the only way back was to move forward. Besides, I was going to be a dad and, as Claire rightly pointed out, being a PC would give me a bit more time and headspace than the stress of the Dog Unit for when our baby was born in March 2011.

On day one in the neighbourhood office, I heard my new boss rallying the troops for my imminent arrival while I hung up my jacket. As I was making my way in, I could hear him explaining I'd been moved off the Dog Unit. I overheard someone say 'It'd better not be that dick off the telly' just as I put my head round the door. It was the sergeant in charge, Rick Warden, and I didn't know at the time but he'd become my best friend.

I spent those first few weeks proving to my colleagues I wasn't the dickhead I had once been and, while I'd been arrogant about the Dog Unit being the best branch of the police, I started to make friends and enjoy working with two-legged creatures rather than ones with four legs. Of course I missed working Riley terribly and, because he was at the prime of his life, he needed a lot of exercise to tire him out and make sure he was happy.

I'd work forty hours a week but spend at least ten more making sure Riley had the exercise he needed.

He settled well into being at home 24/7 to begin with, but I knew him better than he knew himself and soon I started to see slight changes in his behaviour. His recall had always been amazing, in the biggest track with helicopters in the sky and lights flashing everywhere, I could call him and he'd come.

Eight weeks after I started my new job, we were on a long walk on the moors and he ran off. It didn't matter how much I called him, Riley wasn't coming back. With his four legs moving faster than my two, I lost him for a while until he decided to track back to me. I put him in the car and, while I refused to utter the words out loud, a fear I'd had that he was too young to retire proved true. Selfishly, I'd wanted him home with me but, in the prime of his working life, he wasn't ready to be a pet. I would have to live with my mistake, but why should he?

I came home to Claire and said he had to go. She thought I was bluffing – 'You'll never take him, you love him too much. He's like your shadow, you'll never get rid of him.' I told her I'd already put him in the car and that I was taking him to the kennels. At the time, Claire was a few months pregnant and just laughed, convinced I was joking. I gave her one more opportunity to say goodbye but, because she thought I was lying, she kept washing the dishes at the sink.

With tears streaming down my face, I drove my beloved dog to the kennels. We'd spent thousands of hours together, we'd come to the kennels every day to work, we'd caught baddies, saved each other's lives, but I knew taking him home to be my pet had been a selfish move. Riley was at the peak of his career: he had to work, he had so much left to give. He was a police dog, not my pet.

I hugged him and offered him to my friend Heath from the unit, who had just lost his dog – he'd had to be put down because he had inoperable cancer. I asked him to take him, but I was told he had to go out of force. Heath had been on the dogs less time than me and I knew he'd make an amazing handler and do a great job with Riley, but I was told they wouldn't give a dog to another handler because there was a chance I could turn up on the same job as Heath and confuse Riley.

I handed him over knowing I'd never see him again. He'd be someone else's police dog, not mine. I didn't know where he'd be serving or what he'd see, but he'd see out his service saving someone else's life, watching someone else's back. I said my goodbyes crying into his neck while he licked me.

I cried all the way home. I could barely see the road for the tears and it felt like my heart was breaking. There was a physical pain in my chest. I sat outside the house while the tears subsided – I knew Claire didn't feel comfortable when I cried and I didn't want her to know how much I was hurting. When I walked in, she had finished washing the dishes and was putting things away. She gave me one of those smiles of hers that lifted me so much, only this time I felt just felt sorrow and grief so thick, I could barely breathe.

'Get him out then,' she said. But her face changed when she saw I'd been crying: 'Where is he?'

'He's gone, babe.'

'Go and get him back …' She trailed off and I could see she was starting to cry. 'Go and get him back, Gareth …'

As her face folded into tears, I couldn't help her. I was so utterly heartbroken myself, but I knew it was the right thing to do: Riley had to work. It was my stupid fault he'd come off the Dog Unit, but I could give him the chance to get back onto it, albeit a new unit. I might be languishing for years before getting the chance to apply again, but at least I could fast-track Riley back into service, even if that meant I wasn't with him. I loved him as much as I loved Claire and so I had to do what was best for him: he was my top priority. It didn't sit well with me but I had to take myself out of the equation: Riley was in his prime, I had to put what was best for him ahead of what I wanted for myself.

A few days later, I found out he had gone to Hampshire.

The rest of the year dragged, but eventually Christmas came around. Despite my work life not being where I wanted it to be, I adored Claire and planned to ask for her hand in marriage on New Year's Eve. I'd had a ring made and waited for the evening to come.

Her parents always threw a big party because her mum's birthday was on the same night and I had it all planned. Claire's nana and grandad would come over and everyone would be there to celebrate with us. Despite still feeling heavy-hearted about Riley, we had a fantastic night from the second we stepped through the door.

While Claire got Ben sorted with fizzy drinks, I took her dad to one side and asked his permission to marry his only daughter. Luckily, he consented and the stage was set.

We rang in the New Year and Claire's dad made a speech welcoming in 2011. There was a lot of happiness and laughter in the room and I took the opportunity to follow on from him, telling everyone that I wanted to say a few words too. I told Claire how much I loved her and got down on one knee in front of her, asking her if she'd do me the honour of becoming my wife, presenting her with a marquise-cut diamond ring. She said 'yes' and we sealed the deal with a family hug with Ben and Claire's burgeoning tummy with our daughter inside it.

I'd had one of the worst years of my life but it had ended on a high. I desperately hoped it'd set the tone for the fresh start I needed.

Over the next two years, going out on jobs and seeing how the Dog Unit were held in such high regard served as a constant reminder of how much I missed it. Seeing old colleagues coming in with their dogs and doing the job was humiliating and embarrassing, but it was a fuel I needed too. I'd changed completely as a police officer. I dreamt about getting back on the dogs and I knew two things: First, I had to keep my service record pristine. I needed to be the best PC I could be in order to be in with a chance of applying for a position on the dogs, if and when one came up. Second, I knew that if I ever got back on the dogs, I'd never, ever risk being chucked out again.

I'd see friends I'd trained with and they'd be more embarrassed than me when our paths crossed on jobs. I met the lad who'd replaced me a few months afterwards, and when introduced to me his first words were, 'Oh, you're the dickhead I replaced, aren't you?'

I nodded and said I was. 'G' might have kicked off and made a scene but 'G' had ruined my career once. I was sure I'd never, ever let him do it again.

The two years off the Dog Unit proved a huge learning curve for me.

I changed.

I became humble.

I struggled to adapt to work in a team. I'd been solitary with Riley but I found friendships there that I still have and cherish to this day.

I remember one time we were called to a domestic dispute in March 2011. There was a Staffordshire Bull Terrier at the house who'd chased Rick, the sergeant, up the stairs when we arrived. He was scared of dogs and was screaming at me to call the dog or get it off. I couldn't help myself – I found his mania and terror far more amusing than he did.

'I bet you wish you had a dog handler here now, don't you?' I said, laughing before I called the dog. The Staffie was full of hot air but, unless you knew dogs, you wouldn't know that on sight. 'I bet you wish that dickhead handler off the telly was here now to get this dog away from you, don't you?'

He wasn't best pleased but we ended up having a laugh about it afterwards. I'd been solitary for so long, that unit allowed me to make friends and enjoy police work as part of a team.

Shortly after the Staffie incident, we served a warrant and there was a Rottweiler called Demon at the house. We planned to deliver the warrant, find what we were looking for and make the arrest. Demon had other ideas. He was huge – at least 10 stone – and when we started the search and opened a door to the bedroom, this huge beast set about my sergeant, jumping towards him. I got hold of his collar and rushed him into the room behind, using my momentum to get him on his own. He calmed down the second I shut the door and padded down like he wanted to play – his bark had been all bluster and he just wanted some fuss. He wasn't a brave dog, he just guarded the house and made noise.

In the middle of this serious job, Rick came down the landing, asking if the dog was secure. He opened the door to the room that Demon and I were in just as I said, 'I hope you're good at running …' and I let Demon go. I knew he wouldn't harm him, but he gave chase and Rick locked himself in the bathroom, swearing at me: 'If you don't come and get hold of this dog, I'm going to sack you off this unit!' I was laughing my head off and when I called Demon back and put a lead on him, Rick eventually saw the funny side too.

To this day that job remains one that still makes me smile and laugh – it's always one I bring up with Rick when we're out for a pint too. There aren't many times you get a giggle in this line of work so when it does happen, you remember it and hold onto it.

While I enjoyed my life as part of the team, in my heart I was always a dog handler, and any job we went on I relished even more if there was a dog present.

By the start of March 2011, Claire was heavily pregnant. We knew we were having a girl so I'd made good on the first half of my promise and our daughter, Ben's sister, was due any day. We'd got into a routine of going to Claire's parents for Sunday lunch and her dad would talk about handling. I loved hearing his stories and relaying mine with Riley, but it made me miss him and the unit even more. He'd been doing it for over two and a half decades before he retired. His time with the dogs was over and he had no unfinished business. He'd been an incredibly competent and successful handler but my time on the dogs had been taken away from me before I'd been ready to leave so those conversations were always bittersweet.

My weeks as a PC were less stressful than being on the Dog Unit. There was a lightness about me I hadn't had when working the dogs, but I yearned with every fibre of my being to be back at Hough End as a handler. I'd see former colleagues and jobs and, as the initial embarrassment on their part abated, they'd start asking me questions about their dogs or what I'd done with Riley when we'd encountered certain things. A couple of them even asked me to come to Hough End to help with training, something I always agreed to do. I loved being back at my old stamping ground, even though they weren't my dogs and I wasn't part of that team anymore. Being close to it went some way towards sating the desire I had.

I discovered with the birth of Eryn, my Little Bird, there was life outside the dog section. Her birth and becoming a father remain the most amazing experiences of my life.

By the middle of March 2011, Claire was overdue by a week. She'd been for a membrane sweep – a procedure where the midwife tries to stimulate labour – and was understandably tired and uncomfortable. I was exhausted from a long shift. Just as I was falling asleep, I got an elbow in the ribs: 'I've had enough of this, Gareth! I want this baby out and we're going to have to get this baby out the way you got it in, I'm sick of it ...'

I was exhausted but prepared to do my duty when a few seconds later Claire changed colour.

'I don't feel well, Gareth, she's coming!'

How I swore – I was supposed to be back to work in four hours' time. I'd hoped I'd be rested when the baby came and instead I was knackered. We drove and picked up Claire's mum, who'd be with us when Claire delivered. Arriving at the hospital around 1 a.m., I left Claire and her mum at the entrance while I went to park the car. I didn't dawdle and rushed in to see Claire's mum running towards me, shouting at me to hurry up: Claire's waters had broken, she wanted a water birth and the midwife was running it, but things looked like they were happening fast.

At 1.30 a.m., Claire changed colour again and said, 'I need to go to the toilet.' The nurse soon realised Eryn was on her way. Twenty minutes later, my Little Bird was in my arms and I couldn't resist the temptation any more. Kissing Claire on the forehead, I reminded her, 'I told you I'd give you a little girl and a dead easy birth …' It remains the singular most incredible moment of my life. Two hours later, we were home, Claire asleep beside me and my beautiful baby daughter in my arms. It was everything I'd dreamed of. I had two weeks off work and I absolutely doted on my daughter, keeping her in my arms as much as I possibly could. Claire would tell me to put her down and not hold her all the time but

I was beside myself with love. I adored every single thing about being a father and Ben having a sister.

It was the perfect fortnight.

Claire didn't want to go back to work straight away so I said I'd work for both of us and take the overtime I could so she could relax. We had such a strong family unit around us, Claire's parents were close by and a huge hands-on support. I was bringing home both our wages with overtime, which meant Claire could be home with Eryn.

I enjoyed being back at work and the team were all delighted for me, regularly putting up with me prattling on about fatherhood like I was the first bloke in the world to become a dad and proudly showing off new pictures every shift, but being away from Eryn was tough. I'd leave for work when she was asleep and get back after she was already down for the night. I'd spend hours watching her sleep and I took night feeds so I could spend time with her. While she slept, I'd stare at her for hours and she was absolutely perfect in every way.

Something about having Eryn made me yearn for Riley even more than I had before, though. I had his pictures all over the house and Claire even had his photo printed on a mug for me, which I drank my brew out of every day and still do. We were a family, but Riley was missing. I imagined how much he'd dote on this little bundle – the youngest member of our pack – and would have given anything to see them together. Riley was fierce at work but I knew he'd be nurturing towards Eryn. The best police dogs are the ones who have a switch like us handlers do. When the uniform or the harness goes on, when they get in the van, they know they're working, but like us, when the key goes in the front door, they can relax.

Claire had been a PCSO when I met her but she'd gained her stripes and become a fully qualified police officer in 2010. After a fourteen-month maternity leave, she went back to work in 2012. Before Eryn, we'd tried to work similar shifts so our time off could be together but with two children now, we worked opposite shifts so one of us could be home with the kids. It meant we spent less time together as a couple but the kids would have one of us around the majority of the time. We'd talked at length about the sacrifice that would be. It'd mean we'd become Mum and Dad more than Claire and Gareth, but we were both adamant it was what would be best for the kids and we'd have to suck it up and accept the fact our time together as a couple would be limited for the foreseeable future. With hindsight, though, I don't think either of us realised the huge impact our decision would have in the future.

In March 2012, Eryn turned one. We bought her a slide and spent the whole day watching her go down it with the biggest grin on her little face and her giggling like a loon. If she went down the slide once, she must have gone down it two hundred times. She was exhausted by the end of the day and fell asleep a little while after her birthday cake, which her brother Ben dutifully finished off.

Her first year had gone by in the blink of an eye, just as everyone had told me it would. She completed me and filled a part of me I hadn't even known was missing, but while home life was perfect and I was enjoying being a PC, I still held out hope to rejoin the unit I missed.

By September 2012, I'd been off the Dog Unit for over 800 days and still thought of Riley every single day. I'd just finished a night shift when I got a text from a friend on the unit, telling me a job would be available. My heart flew into my mouth and I felt sick and excited at the same time. I didn't dare to dream but instantly got excited before I went into panic mode. In the two and a half years I'd been off the unit, I'd always held out hope I could get back onto it when a vacancy became available. What if I applied and didn't get it? Until then, it had always been a possibility. I could spend my time longing to be back on the unit because it was still a glimmer on the horizon – applying and failing hadn't entered my head.

Determined to do things the right way round this time, I asked my direct boss if I could get the green light to apply and also asked the seniors on the Dog Unit if I could. They all said 'yes' and I've never worked as hard on anything as I did my application. The inspector I'd told to fuck off had to interview me for the job so I knew I was up against it and would have to prove myself. They'd left the door ajar when I'd been kicked off, telling me I could apply again, so while I'd left under a very dark, very black, very ominous cloud, I hoped it would have dissipated by the time I filled in my application form. Besides, I was a different person to the one who'd been chucked out. 'G' had been obnoxious, arrogant, egotistical and a bit of a git. Gareth had more experience now of working with people as well as animals. I knew what it felt like to take a risk and lose, and I swore if I got the job I'd never take it for granted and never, ever think I was bigger than the unit and my colleagues again.

I'd be Gareth, not 'G', and be an even better handler than I'd been with Riley.

There were four slots the unit had to fill, and on the day of the interview Claire was as nervous as me. I felt sick, I was shaking like a leaf and I couldn't eat all morning. Claire came with me and waited in the car to try and still my nerves.

I knew the second the interview finished, though, that I had the job and I don't say that in arrogance. I was able to really show the panel that I was a different person to the one they'd kicked out: I had the experience, I knew that already, but I'd also been kicked out and had learned so much and was able to get all of that across.

Seven days after I walked out of the interview, I received the call: I was back on the unit.

I was a Greater Manchester Police dog handler again.

6

I BROKE DOWN IN TEARS when I got the call. It felt like I'd become myself again, the part of me that had been missing was back and I swore I'd never let it go again. Claire was delighted for me and while Eryn didn't understand what all the fuss was about, she giggled in delight when I threw her up in the air to celebrate. I was shaking again but this time with excitement, not nerves.

Once my tears had subsided, and my voice stopped wobbling, I called Paul Quinlan, who would be my trainer again and asked what dogs we had. I was like a child at Christmas, desperate to know what dog I was going to get. He told me he was picking up some new puppies from a breeder we used that day and to come and have a look the next day when they were in.

To say I didn't sleep a wink with excitement is an understatement. I was buzzing when I arrived at the kennels the next morning – I hadn't even managed my morning brew, I was so excited.

Paul had contacts all over the country and the breeder he'd been with when I'd called was one of the best in the country. His dogs were all fantastic and he was incredibly experienced. When he'd found out the day before I was back on the unit, there was one specific dog Paul wanted for me, but the breeder had been keen to keep this particular pup for himself. Being persuasive and on my side, Paul did a number on him, explained my situation, what I'd been through and how long I'd waited to get back on the unit.

That juvenile dog was Theo.

Barely able to contain my excitement, I went into the kennels. There was a new Dutch Herder called Shadow and some other really beautiful dogs. I walked straight past Theo the first time I saw him, completely unaware of what Paul had planned for me. I'd heard about Shadow – the talk of the kennels, he would be going to an experienced handler (me, I hoped). Fourteen months old and stunning, he was such a piece of kit.

Paul came in and saw me admiring him: 'What you doing, Gareth? That's not your dog, you're having Theo.'

'What?'

I'd presumed I'd be a natural choice for Shadow and had barely noticed the German Shepherd a few kennels back down the line.

'Trust me, you're having Theo.'

You don't argue with Paul at the best of times and I had a lot of ground to make up and was the new boy again, so I nodded my head and walked back down to Theo's kennel. Sat in the corner of his kennel, he was looking like his world had fallen apart. He'd been the breeder's dog until twenty-four hours ago. Now he'd been put somewhere completely new with scents he didn't recognise and a cacophony of noise. He wasn't barking and I could tell he wasn't naturally aggressive.

As a handler, you want a dog that's barking: it's a sign of communication and something you can work with. The quiet ones, you don't know what they're thinking. They can have nervous aggression, which means they could snap.

Theo was sat there, right at the back, just looking at me. He had a way about him and I instantly felt like he was looking straight through me and into my soul. I hadn't had a police dog in two years and gently let myself into his kennel – he was no Simba or Riley and I wanted to let him guide the pace of our introduction.

I sat on the floor on the opposite side of the kennel and for ten minutes he wouldn't come near me. He paced up and down and I could tell he was stressed. The breeder had owned him until yesterday and here he was in a noisy, unfamiliar kennel surrounded by barking dogs. His world had fallen apart and he was trying to be brave and adjust – I knew how he felt. He eventually came over to me and put his head against my head. I tickled him under the chin and we both exhaled at exactly the same time.

In that second, I knew he was my dog.

'Me and you are going to be fine, young man, I promise.'

He started wagging his tail and our bond was formed: it felt like we'd both had a bad time but, together, we could fix each other.

When I took him home, Claire was just as crazy about him as I was. He was absolutely stunning. I put him in the kennel enclosure I'd had at home which had been Riley's and sat with him for hours. I told him everything that had happened; I told him about Rufus and Denver and how I'd always wanted to work with dogs. I told him about Simba and Riley and getting kicked off the unit.

'You're my way back,' I told him. 'We can make such a difference if we learn to trust each other. We can be something, Theo, we really can.'

I was determined to get back what I'd lost and I knew I couldn't do it without Theo. I needed him to know how important he was and how much I needed him.

When I went out later to take him for a walk, he came to heel at my side instantly. While his behaviour was amazing, it saddened me too. He hadn't learned to be a dog. He'd been taught by an exceptional breeder and he was clearly bright because he'd learned so many commands and had set behaviours but his essence needed to be restored: he needed to learn to be a dog again. In all his training, though – and he was a spectacularly trained puppy – he hadn't been exposed to things so many dogs had. Not only was I going to have to train him to be a police dog, I would have to teach him how to be a dog.

The first time he saw a car drive past, he cowered. He was also scared of sheets drying on the line, loud noises and scared of Eryn too: he had no life experience. He'd been raised so far to be a fantastic specimen of his breed, but outside of the rural kennels he'd been born into he didn't know how to function.

Claire changed her mind on his promise and brilliance the second she saw him hiding at the back of his kennel as our bed sheets dried in the wind: 'Gareth, he's a beautiful dog, don't get me wrong, but he won't make a police dog. He's scared of his own shadow.'

As he'd spend years leaping to my defence, I instantly jumped to his: 'He's not, Claire, he just needs to learn. You wait, you'll see ...'

Claire's dad said the same thing. He was complimentary too, saying Theo looked the part, but he wasn't sure he'd make a police dog.

Like me, though, Eryn fell for him straight away. By now, she was eighteen months old and we introduced them to each other slowly – I'd give him one of her baby grows to get him used to her scent. We had big patio doors, and Eryn would sit in her rocker looking at him and he'd sit and watch her. It was as if he knew she was the littlest member of our pack, the one we all doted on and rallied round.

I knew there was something about him – he was only young but a wise soul and the way he'd looked at me when we first met was how he kept looking at me, as if he could see right through to the core of me. It felt like he'd been sent here to put me back together. We needed each other and, from the second he lay his head against mine in that noisy kennel block, I knew our bond would last forever. He'd listened diligently while I'd told him my backstory and how we'd ended up with each other. His head had lain on my lap as I sat in his kennel in the garden, telling him about Rufus and Riley. He hadn't been bored or padded away to take a nap, he got me – he got me like Riley had never done.

I also knew the old Gareth wouldn't have taken Theo on, but I'd changed.

Theo was a different dog from Riley from the second I got him. Riley didn't need me, he protected me because it was his job. Theo would grow to protect me because he loved me. For the first few weeks, though, I was the only one rooting for him. He was home while we got used to each other and then the course started in November 2012.

Day one was bite work. I had to train him with the sleeve to bite into it and hold. It's how we'd detain criminals and one of the most fundamental parts of being a police dog. We knew Theo could bite – his breeder had taught him to – but we didn't know how successfully he could do it or what type of grip he'd have. The minute I saw him bite, I got so excited, but it scared me too: he wouldn't come off.

As a dog handler, your dog learning and listening to the 'out' command is as important as the command to bite itself. Every police dog needs an 'out' and that command has to be set in stone. We're there to detain and harm sometimes comes along with that, but unreasonable force from a police dog should never be used. I knew Theo was amazing but I also knew I'd have to work hard to make sure his 'out' was set in stone before he started working for real. He was amazing, though, and I knew when we got that bit sorted and when we started policing together as a team, no one would get away from us.

Over the coming weeks, as I trained him and as he developed, I didn't want to come home – I would have done back-to-back shifts with him training if they'd let me. I was fascinated seeing his progress and honoured to be a part of it. I was buzzing at Theo's potential and couldn't wait to get us on the streets – I knew we could make a difference and help people. It started to feel like I'd never been away – everything came back to me and it felt so right and familiar driving to the kennels every day. I'd learned so much from my time off the unit, but being back felt like I was where I should be, like I was home.

While Theo's bite work was something else, there's a part of training we do called a 'long walk', where we take our dogs out for around sixteen miles to check their stamina and introduce them to different terrains. When a job comes in, it could be urban or it might be farmland or moor, so they need to be comfortable on all terrains. It could also be a short track of a half-mile and take twenty to thirty minutes or it might be miles and take up to seven or eight hours. The dogs need to know what's expected of them and handlers need to know they have to put in the miles and the hours in all weathers when they're asked to.

Theo was terrified of the woods, scared of heather and the unfamiliar noises and smells, but he persevered and did amazingly. By the time the long walk was over, two weeks into our training, in my heart and head he'd surpassed Riley. I loved Riley and had a bond with him, but Theo was on another level. I didn't need to protect Riley, he protected me, but I felt protective over Theo and I think that gave us an edge.

By the time I finished work for Christmas 2012, I knew he'd make an incredible police dog. That Christmas was perfect. I was back doing the job I'd longed for, I knew my partner would be one of the most incredible police dogs Greater Manchester Police would ever have and family life was pretty perfect too. To say I was feeling quite proud of myself when I took Theo out for a walk on Christmas Eve would be an understatement. The house looked perfect, all the presents were wrapped and I was looking forward to an amazing festive period. We started our usual morning walk, both with a spring in our steps, and were enjoying the cold weather and clear skies. We went into the woods and Theo was mooching about in the leaves like normal when his head came up. I knew he had the scent of something and the next thing I saw was the back of his tail as he disappeared through the woods.

I called him back and while his recall was amazing, he'd been entranced by the scent and within about ten seconds, I couldn't see or hear him. I decided to stay where I was and wait for him to come back. Five minutes went by, ten minutes went by ... Watching the minutes tick away on my watch and using all my senses, I strained to see or hear anything that could give an indication of where he might be or where he'd darted off to. There was nothing, though, no sound, no noise, no sight of him.

I started to sweat and panic. I'd been kicked off the Dog Unit in 2010. I'd just got back on and been told in no uncertain terms not to mess up again, and now I'd lost an unlicensed police dog in the woods on Christmas Eve, who knew how to bite.

I felt sick, but I tried to stay calm. Theo was a softie out of training but he wasn't the finished article and I was still getting to know him. Without me to help him see how he should react to things, I had no idea what he'd get up to.

Twenty-five minutes went by and I was screaming and shouting his name to no avail. Distraught, I buried my face in my hands. When I lifted my head, though, Theo was right there: breathless, tail wagging, big smile on his face. He was covered in mud, but looking very proud of himself.

The second he saw my face, though, his changed and he ducked his head, looking at the ground. He knew he was in trouble and so he put on his best meek face, but it didn't wash. I put him straight on his lead and all the way home I told him off. I was in the midst of telling him he couldn't ever do that to me again when we were stopped by another walker, who told me he'd seen Theo chasing deer, lolloping around with them and generally having the time of his life. While I tried to stay mad with him, I couldn't. Everything he did made me smile, even when I was cross with him. Claire found the whole story hilarious when I got back and couldn't stop laughing about it all day.

Our first Christmas as a family with Theo was amazing. I let him out before the kids opened their presents, then Theo opened his: he had a new lead, a new ball and some chew sticks. I walked him, then we had our first Christmas meal – on Christmas Day, he always has what we have and he loved every morsel.

Four weeks later, at the end of January 2013, we passed the course. He wasn't the star of the show – a dog called Bomber got that honour – but Theo had great traits and some that we needed to work on. His bite was amazing, but he wasn't so good at tracking. A lot of it came down to pressure: you train them to track and you don't talk to them while they're tracking. You let them concentrate on what they're doing, but that didn't work for Theo – I could tell it didn't, but protocol is protocol and I was the new kid again and didn't want to mess up.

No matter how often we tried, though, when I stopped talking to him, he'd get stressed and panic and lose the track. It was like he worried he was doing something wrong and then he'd lie on the floor and shut down. Little by little, I realised he needed support while tracking and from then on his tracking came on massively. I'd whisper to him while he was tracking, 'Good lad, that's it! Well done, Theo, you're doing great, son!' It seemed to help him and with his confidence restored, he got better and better at tracking.

The powers that be would have frowned upon it if they'd known but I was able to quietly reassure Theo he was a good lad and doing a good job so we went unnoticed, under the radar.

Life was as perfect as it could have been: Theo was fantastic, Eryn was everything I dreamt of, I was back on the dogs … Eryn would come for walks with me all the time, her bond with Theo was growing, she'd help me muck out the kennels and sit on my shoulders when her little legs couldn't cope with the long moorland walks we'd go on. Theo would try and join in carrying Eryn and would pick her up gently by the hood of her waterproof onesie. He'd carry her around like she was his and she'd be giggling like mad at the thought of being one of Theo's pups while he'd be proud of himself, thinking he was carrying her just like I did. He was so gentle with her. It was as if he knew I was looking after him so he looked after what I loved.

Nothing could go wrong, it seemed.

Eryn was obsessed with pegs in the peg basket – she'd run around the garden, throwing them one by one on the grass. Theo would follow her patiently, picking each peg up in his mouth and returning it to the basket. It was their little game: I hadn't taught either of them to do it, they'd figured it out for themselves and it didn't matter how often they played it, neither of them ever got bored.

Theo passed out at the start of 2013 and hit the ground running. On our first shift, despite having been silent and not a barker during training, he howled like mad at sirens. He also howled the first time I put our blue lights in the van on. It made me laugh, but I knew eventually it would get annoying and distracting, and while I'd work to train it out of him, to this day he still howls at ambulances.

Within weeks on the job, though, he had his first bite.

It was February 2013. We were called to someone attempting to break in. Instantly, I felt like we had something to prove: I was a different person, but could Gareth make it on the Dog Unit as well as 'G' had?

The expectation on myself was huge.

I got Theo on the lead and went round the back of the house. He didn't know what he was doing; he knew his training but real life is different and he wasn't at Hough End any more. It was dark, around 2 a.m., and while the moon cast some light, there was a lot of darkness. I could make out a caravan in the darkness and Theo signalled there was someone there.

Theo was still on his lead but as we rounded the corner, we could see someone running away towards the main road down an alleyway. I kept Theo on his lead and we gave chase. Adrenaline was surging through me and while part of it felt familiar – after all, I'd done this hundreds of times before – there was a huge unknown quantity in that the dog at the end of the lead wasn't Riley who I knew inside out, it was Theo who'd aced training, but could he cut it in the real world?

When we were within 10 metres of the lad who was running like he'd left the oven on at home, I issued the challenges. I hadn't uttered them in years but they were on the tip of my tongue and came out exactly as they had before.

Clearly thinking he could outrun us, the lad ignored the challenges and I gave Theo the command to hold him. The next few seconds happened in slow motion and it felt like I didn't breathe. It was the ultimate test. I had no idea how Theo was going to respond or what he was going to do.

When all police dogs come out of training, it can be hard to get them to bite in a real-life scenario. They're used to biting a thick material sleeve – for them, it's a toy – but human skin is different and you do get some who refuse to bite. Not Theo, though – he set off like a rocket. I stopped to watch and he got the lad exactly where he should within a couple of seconds.

I caught up, gave the 'out' command for Theo to release and he did exactly as he was told, returned to my side and seemed relieved. I was so happy but didn't show it. I made the arrest and handed the lad over to the attending police officers while Theo and I made our way the few minutes' walk back to the van.

I'd barely put Theo in the van and given him some water when I was physically sick. The adrenaline that had fired had given way to nausea on the way back and while I made sure I was out of everyone's eyeline to avoid the inevitable teasing that would happen if anyone saw me, I was sick as the proverbial dog.

Once everything was out, though, I couldn't stop beaming.

He'd done it. Not only had he done it, he'd aced it!

I instantly thought about Riley's first bite, not to compare them but I'd been just as nervous and Riley had done a great job but Theo was excellent, like he was born to do it. I couldn't wipe the smile off my face and fussed him like mad.

He was excited because I was excited but I could see he was confused too. He'd simply done what he did in training, what he'd been doing for weeks. Now he kept looking at me – he could sense and see I was so excited and elated – but it was like he didn't see what all the fuss was about.

I'd spent two years away from what I'd always wanted and was finally back with a dog that I adored – I had redemption.

7

WHILE THEO AND RILEY were such different dogs, that same bond, the instant connection and chemistry, was so strong with Theo, just as it had been with Riley. I'd been a different handler when I had Riley and he'd been the dog I needed back then. With Theo, I was older and wiser and not so gung-ho, and he read that in me. We fitted one another perfectly.

What I'd been told as a handler when I first started about whatever you feel going right down the lead and into your dog had been borne out, and Theo and I started to become alike in exactly the same way as Riley and I had been very similar. Within the first few shifts, Theo started to lie in exactly the same spot, in exactly the same position, as Riley had. There was a tenderness with Theo that Riley hadn't had, though. Theo was a fantastic police dog and I knew he'd have an outstanding career ahead of him, but Riley had done what he'd done because he wanted to, because he had a bit of an ego, just as I'd had, whereas Theo did everything because he wanted to please and protect me. I felt exactly the same way about him.

Theo wasn't even two when he made his first bite and he wouldn't retire until he was eight and a half. We had six and a half years of cleaning-up to do – it felt incredible. That year, we went from strength to strength.

After a pretty average shift in the middle of February 2013, I came home excited about the day ahead. Claire and I had just seven weeks to go until we got married, and we'd planned to spend the day finalising a few details and running some errands we needed to get sorted ahead of our big day. Her hen do was the next day and I'd have the kids while she enjoyed a much-needed night out with her girlfriends before we became Mr and Mrs Greaves.

I was still in uniform and I'd picked Claire and Eryn up so we could make the last post at the post office and get back in time to get Ben from school. Eryn was strapped into her car seat and babbling away about something or other, but fell quiet when we got to a set of traffic lights. Claire and I were in the front and Claire asked her a question she didn't answer. She turned around to see if she'd fallen asleep – we were only a few hundred metres from the house but Eryn loved falling asleep in her car seat. But rather than give her a stroke and put a jumper around our Little Bird while she snoozed, Claire started screaming. A piercing scream, a sound I'd never ever heard her make before.

I looked in the rear-view mirror and didn't recognise Eryn. Her eyes were rolled back in her head and she was fitting, her little body convulsing, going limp and then rigid as she writhed around in her car seat, thrashing against the straps that were supposed to keep her safe. I've seen a lot of things I'd un-see if I could, but that image, the instant helplessness, is forged into my memory forever. Despite the traffic light being red, I blasted the horn and ran every single red light until we got to the local hospital, a few miles away. Thankfully, it was the middle of the day and the roads were quiet. We arrived within a few minutes and I dumped the car in an ambulance bay, unstrapping Eryn and running inside with her in my arms. She'd stopped fitting and come round a little but was extremely confused and very lethargic too. She was admitted instantly and put onto a monitor while medics tried to figure out what had happened to her.

Eryn was confused and upset; she didn't know what had happened or where she was. It was unfamiliar and it scared her, but we tried to keep her calm. We both wanted to panic and scream and cry but we did our best to keep things together and not show her just how frightened we were. Claire would excuse herself for a few minutes to cry, then pull herself back together again and plaster a smile on her face so our little girl didn't know just how terrified she was.

Eryn was given a cannula for fluids but screamed and cried a lot because it hurt her. Claire was in pieces – it was like all the pain Eryn was going through, she felt too. I felt hopeless, unable to make anything better for either of them.

We'd been teaching Eryn to count to ten and, with the cannula in, fluids on board, blood taken and a scan arranged, she started to calm down. We did everything we could to distract her so decided to keep practising numbers and counting to ten. Our Little Bird got to number four before the same thing happened again and she started convulsing. This time out of her car seat the seizure was even more intense, her little body at the behest of whatever was going on inside her without the straps of the seat to limit her movement. Her eyes rolled back in her head and both Claire and I filled with terror at what was happening to our daughter.

'Please, someone come and help my little girl!' I was

shouting, but I didn't care. We'd been placed in a cubicle while we were monitored and because we'd been alone when Eryn started fitting the second time, I was desperate for someone to come and help, someone to make it all go away and give us our healthy girl back.

Doctors and nurses filled Eryn with wide-spectrum antibiotics, a course of treatment they hoped would help, even though they didn't know what they were looking at. They couldn't confirm anything and all the tests they were doing had so far come back inconclusive. There's one thing worse than being in hospital with your child convulsing and that's being told by medical professionals that no one knows what it is. The staff were amazing and reassured us they were doing everything they could to diagnose, but not knowing what you're looking at when your child is sick is almost as scary as knowing what they've got. Claire and I were dumbstruck: held in a limbo with no idea what was happening to our daughter. Eryn was sedated while the antibiotics took hold and tried to get rid of whatever was hurting her. There were more tests planned, which we were told would hopefully yield an answer.

I've seen bad people put in prison, I've had threats on my life and I've had a proper seeing-to by some very strong people, but nothing in my life has ever been as terrifying as watching my Little Bird, my daughter, my Eryn, convulsing and me not being able to do a thing about it.

An hour or two after the antibiotics were administered, a doctor came in and told us it could be meningitis.

The 'M' word.

The one no parent ever wants to hear.

Instantly, I thought about the news reports you see where children have lost legs or arms or both because of the condition. Sick to the pit of my stomach, I almost collapsed and it was all I could do not to throw up, there and then.

An hour or so later, with Eryn more comfortable and Claire on the phone to her mum and dad, I called my sister Suzanne in New Zealand. She was on the other side of the world but she was a doctor so I explained what had happened. She confirmed my worst fears, telling me it could be meningitis because Eryn had no temperature at all. She reassured me we were in the right place and that the medics would do everything they could to get a diagnosis and treatment. Suzanne was reassured they'd already started antibiotics but I'd called her hoping she'd say it was nothing, that it was something every kid went through that I'd missed out on hearing about at the antenatal classes, but she couldn't make it better either.

As the antibiotics kicked in and Eryn slept, we decided Claire would stay at the hospital while I went home to take care of Ben and Theo. Ben had been with Claire's mum and dad and Theo was at home in his kennel so both needed to be sorted. We came up with a plan, which consisted of putting Theo into kennels at work and leaving Ben with Claire's parents so we could both be with Eryn as much as possible.

I got home as fast as I could and packed Theo up, explaining to him what had happened as I got his things together. On the way to the kennels I called work, relaying what I'd told Theo and Claire. My boss was shocked and clearly upset for me but told me not to even think about Theo. I knew he'd be in safe hands with work and the reassurance was just what I needed, so I said a fast goodbye to him and then spent the next week in hospital. I'd be at the kennels with Theo when I could, checking on him at least once a day, but Claire barely left Eryn's hospital room unless she absolutely had to. Every night she slept a couple of hours sitting next to Eryn's bed and would spend hours watching her sleep.

It was without a doubt one of the worst times of my life.

Eryn would come round, then sleep, then wake up and then sleep again. She had so little energy, but little by little it returned. The periods of wakefulness went on for longer, she was a million miles away from being back to her old self, but at least the convulsions had stopped. Of course we were delighted they'd stopped, but it felt as if we were still in some kind of minefield or no man's land. No one could give us any answers or tell us when Eryn would get better or when life could go back to normal. Every question we asked was met with the answer that tests so far had been inconclusive but there were more they could try. Meningitis was discounted after a few days, which of course was a huge relief, but was then replaced by possible epilepsy, which was just as terrifying in a completely different way.

Eryn was discharged after eight days but we didn't get a diagnosis: they couldn't confirm what it was. While she hadn't fitted for over a week, on her first day home Claire and I were on eggshells.

What if it happened again?

What if she swallowed her tongue this time?

What if there was something lurking that was worse than what had happened before?

What if the medics had missed something?

We tried to keep all our fears from her, but they felt thick and heavy and inside we were drowning.

Ben was delighted to have Eryn home, and on her first day back in her own bed she slept for fourteen hours straight. Claire and I checked on her every twenty minutes to make sure she was still breathing and was doing okay.

Eryn was home but with Theo still in kennels, it didn't feel as though everything was back as it should be. Over the next few days, though, as Eryn got better, I got worse.

I wasn't coping very well with what had happened, I was anxious and I wasn't sleeping or eating much. I'd wake in the night and spend hours staring at her sleeping like I had when she was a newborn baby. I was so worried it would happen again at any point and not getting a diagnosis just made everything worse, it was all so open-ended.

Claire was struggling too: neither of us had ever encountered anything like that in our lives and we'd spend hours each in our own worlds trying to process what had happened.

Theo came home a few hours after Eryn did. I knew I needed him to help me deal with it. Just his presence was soothing to me; it always has been. Without him I don't feel complete: it's as if when we're apart something is missing. I needed him back like I needed both my hands.

He was delighted to be home and Eryn was delighted to see him but it was like he sensed something seismic had happened. He'd usually bound up to Eryn and he was clearly delighted to see her but he knew now wasn't the time for play and so he rested his head on her lap while she fussed him.

Weeks of tests followed but no resolution was ever given. Eryn wasn't diagnosed with anything and the tests were inconclusive. We were told it could have been a one-off that would never happen again or it might be that the same thing happened at some other time in her childhood or life. We could have lived with a diagnosis, tried to work around it, but not knowing was horrible. Would it happen tomorrow? In ten minutes from now, or never, ever again? We didn't know and no one could tell us.

I went back to work with Theo a week after Eryn came home from hospital. She'd gone from being the ill, tired little girl we'd brought home to our normal Little Bird. Now she had her bags of energy back, was happily counting to ten and, to look at her, you'd never have known what had happened. I still worried about her and watched her sleep when I wasn't working, but Theo had been hugely important in helping me cope. I'd had enough of the ones I loved being in pain and getting back to work with him was the tonic I needed.

There are several scenarios for which you can never train a police dog and one of them is getting hurt. Theo would experience plenty of others in his service but the first harsh lesson he had to learn was that he wasn't invincible. Until now, he'd been the one who had done the hurting on his jobs; he himself had never come to any harm. Inevitably, in our line of work at some point he was going to get injured.

In April that year, we were called to a burglary. It was a textbook job and I issued challenges to a man who was running away from the scene. When he ignored me and kept running, I sent Theo in. He caught him with his usual bite on the arm but before the man went down, he was able to kick Theo really hard in the ribs. I heard the dull thud followed by Theo's whimper, something I'd never heard before.

Within a second or two, I was with them but when I gave Theo the command to release and went to put him back on his lead, he bit me on the hand because he was scared and hadn't ever been hurt before. I wasn't angry with him at all; it happens when you work in such close proximity together. Riley had done it too, but Theo was such a powerful dog he went in a bit deeper than I'd have liked and I had to pop to hospital to get it checked out.

While Theo waited for me in the van, I wasn't the only one in A&E that night with a dog bite. The lad Theo had latched onto needed his wound checked too but I made sure I steered clear of him while we were both checked. Though Theo and I both turned out alright, he learned the hard way that sometimes the people we catch fight back – something he'd learn more over the years to come.

I got home past 7 a.m., got Theo sorted in his kennel, went and made myself a cup of tea, and sat in his kennel with him, where we debriefed on the day's events. From that shift on, we'd follow the same ritual: I'd sit on the floor, he'd lay his head on my lap and listen while I told him what we'd done right and what we needed to work on.

'Good job there, son, you did well, but this … [I let him sniff my thumb] this isn't going to fly. We can't be going about our work if you're going to bite your dad.'

Theo was never my police dog, he was an equal partner.

While I tried to sleep that day, I spent a lot of time tossing and turning, thinking about how much Theo meant to me. I'd instantly seen red when I heard that kick hit Theo. I'd felt my heart skip a beat and the adrenaline flow when I'd heard his whimper. I know the dogs are generally considered a piece of kit by the force but, to anyone who handles them, they're more than that. I kept telling myself I'd done well not to land the lad a punch when he'd hurt my dog but, in reality, I knew I'd have to keep my temper in check when it came to Theo being hurt.

I call Theo my son. He doesn't get paid for what he does, he does it out of loyalty to me. It's more than just a love and protection, it's a feeling of being inseparable. Whenever we're together and not working, he has to be touching me. If we're in the same room, he won't lie in front of the fire, he'll lie with his head on my foot or his paw on my leg. We've got each other's back in a way no ordinary dog and his owner can experience. Toe to toe, we head into the fray together. It's a camaraderie that exists in combat between soldiers – we've seen so much together, been hurt, faced down danger. Our relationship is more equal than simply being an owner, so it's hard to stay calm when he's hurt, something that would be tested hugely in our future.

8

Ben's always been a good lad. From the minute he sat on my knee when I first met him, he's been a really good boy with a big heart. He's always had a great relationship with his own dad, yet he accepted me as his stepdad and we grew closer and closer. He was a fantastic big brother to Eryn, really nurturing and kind. As he grew, he turned into an amazing sportsman too. There was nothing he couldn't turn his hand to, it seemed, but like most northern lads of a certain age, Ben lived for football.

He supported Manchester United, was on the books at Manchester City and he loved the Beautiful Game. He'd be in the house or the garden with a football all the time. He played on the same team as his cousins and never missed training. You might have had to nag him to get his homework done but he'd be ready for training half an hour before you had to leave: boots done up, water bottle ready, desperate to get out on the pitch and play the game he adored.

It was nearly the end of March 2013 and Claire and I were weeks away from making things official. She had rearranged the hen do she'd had to cancel when Eryn was in hospital and there was barely anything else left to sort for our wedding. Ben was now aged ten and, as usual, he was ready for training. He was tall and a cracking centre-forward. I dropped him off at the ground and planned to take Theo for a walk while he was at training. After forty-five minutes, I came back to watch the final few minutes of training and my brother-in-law was there watching Ben's cousins. He hadn't called me, but when I went over to say hello, he told me he was worried about Ben.

'There's something wrong with him, he's not acting right ...'

I called Ben over: 'You okay, son?'

'I don't feel well, Dad,' he told me.

It was a cold night so I asked him if he wanted to sit out for a bit. He sat out but started to slur his words. His pupils began to dilate and I knew something wasn't right: my first thought was that someone had spiked his drink.

I got him in the car and was chatting to him, but he started to get really vague. Nothing he was saying made sense:

'You alright, Ben? I'm starting to worry about you, son.'

'Green ... Blue ...'

Something was happening to him and everything I'd felt with Eryn came rushing back. I was trying not to panic, telling myself some lads had just put a bit of alcohol in his bottle or something, or that he might have a bit of concussion from heading the ball. I called Claire and said I was taking him to A&E. I told her not to worry and that I'd call her soon.

We got to the hospital, and while Ben was still awake he was slurring his speech and had no idea who I was. It was terrifying. He was conscious but I could see he was going downhill fast. I left the car in the ambulance bay with a note so I could get him straight in and I carried him to A&E.

I was giving his details to the receptionist when he threw up all over me. They rushed him through but it occurred to me instantly I didn't have parental consent for him and I was the only one with him. I called Claire and said she needed to get there fast. She arrived within minutes and, the second she walked in, Ben had a massive fit. Claire started crying her eyes out, terrified – we'd been here just weeks before with Eryn. I hugged her and said I'd phone Ben's biological dad. When he was on his way, I told Claire to stay with Ben while I took Theo home, who was sat in the car. I told her I'd get him home and then visit her mum and dad to tell them more of what was going on. Claire had called them over in a panic to sit with Eryn while she came to the hospital and they were at home, worried sick about what had happened to their grandson.

I got home, sorted Theo and told them what little I knew. Claire had been a single mum with Ben for years; they were like another set of parents to him. They'd helped raise him while she worked as a PCSO and built a career for herself. I promised I'd update them every few minutes when I went back to the hospital and, after changing out of my sick-covered clothes, I headed back up.

I was so panicked at the thought of Claire being there on her own and going through it without me beside her, I drove faster than I should have done to get back to her and Ben. On the way back I was pulled over for speeding, but when I explained to the traffic officers what was happening, they asked if I wanted their blue lights to help me get there faster.

The force is like a big family and, when one of us needs help, we all mobilise. Having come from a bit of a dysfunctional family unit in my youth, it's something that drew me to the force in the first place and remains one of the things I most love about it.

I knew something must be seriously wrong with Ben because of how quickly he'd gone downhill, but no one could tell us what had happened or why. It was like being with Eryn again – the worst had happened but we had no answers.

Ben's dad had arrived while I'd been away updating Claire's parents and so I took a step back: my role now was to support Claire. I loved Ben more than anything but his biological dad had precedence and he was just as worried as Claire.

Ben was sedated while they ran a battery of tests and did an MRI scan. While with Eryn we'd been there for days without an answer, but just three hours after we first walked in, the doctors told us Ben had a massive bleed on the brain. I'd thought with Eryn a diagnosis would have been a relief, that not knowing was worse and being able to go from there would help. But knowing ten-year-old Ben – who looked so small and vulnerable – not only had a bleed on his brain, but a big one too, was horrendous.

Claire and Ben's dad were ushered away by doctors while the next steps were explained and I made my way to the canteen to get us all a coffee. Ben was blue-lit to the Royal Manchester Children's Hospital, twenty minutes away from the Tameside, the hospital I'd taken him to.

I sorted Ben's dad's car with enough parking (he had given me the key) and went home to get Claire clothes and check on Eryn. When I got to the hospital again, though, Claire told me to go home, rest and take care of Eryn, then come back in the morning.

With Eryn fast asleep and my son in hospital, sleep didn't come easy and I spent most of the night sat in the garden with Theo in his kennel. I told him everything that had happened; told him about Ben's training, him being sick, all of it.

'Look, mate, I'm sorry but you're going to have to go into kennels at work again. I know you don't want to, but I'm going to have to get you picked up too – I can't drop you in there myself because Eryn's sleeping.'

I called the night shift and Theo was picked up. He didn't want to get in the van, but he went with some encouragement from me and I promised I'd come to him as soon as I could.

It sounds daft, but I felt split three ways. Eryn was sleeping and still recovering herself, Ben was in hospital and I was terrified he could get worse before he got better, and I'd let Theo down by putting him at the bottom of the priority list.

After a sleepless night, I went up to the hospital first thing.

Around 9 a.m. on the Easter bank holiday weekend, Ben was diagnosed with a brain tumour. They couldn't say whether it was cancerous – they wouldn't know until they operated.

Claire's knee-jerk reaction was 'I'm getting married in two weeks ...' before she burst into tears, but the damage was done and she and Ben's dad had an argument. She hadn't meant it at all in the way it sounded, she wasn't bothered at all about our big day and neither was I. Ben was the priority, but understandably her words weren't received how she'd intended.

Ben was scheduled for an operation which would tell us how serious his condition was and whether the tumour was malignant. We were told we could take him home for a couple of days to spend some time together as a family and bring him back for the surgery.

Ben was awake and feeling okay. He had very little recollection of what had happened at training and we sugar-coated it so he wasn't scared. Between Claire and Ben's dad, they made the decision not to tell him about the operation, or what he might be looking at.

Ben came home for the weekend knowing he had to be taken into hospital again for some more treatment, where he'd be put to sleep. All the way home in the car, he kept talking about the fact it was Eryn's birthday and how happy he was to be home so he could celebrate it with her. Both Claire and I tried not to fall apart in the front, both in awe of how brave and selfless he was being.

When we got home, I went to the kennels to get Theo. Claire and I had talked in the kitchen when we got Ben home about how we needed to try and make Eryn's birthday as happy as possible. We also agreed to cancel the wedding – we'd take a financial hit on it, but that was the least of our concerns given what we were dealing with.

That weekend, we made the relevant calls and gave Eryn a family birthday party with lots of cake and balloons. She was in her element and Ben fussed her just as much as we all did. Seeing them together, happy and having fun, was wonderful and both Claire and I took as many pictures of the two of them as we could. We didn't know what the future held for Ben and, while we were both at our wits' end with worry, playing happy families and pretending everything was normal for Eryn's birthday was tough, but probably what we all needed. Had it not been for Little Bird, I know we'd have spent the weekend with lots of tears, worrying ourselves sick. As it was, we smiled, laughed and ate a lot of cake.

While I'd only been off work for a few days, I'd have given anything to have put my uniform on and gone and worked a shift with my partner. My world at home felt like it was spiralling out of control. Both the children I adored had been gravely ill within a matter of weeks of one another. The wedding which was supposed to be the start of my own happily ever after wasn't happening, I didn't know which way was up and nothing was predictable. Worst of all, I was utterly helpless. There wasn't anything I could do to secure an outcome or make everything okay again: no bravery, no nous, no quick thinking would do anything.

We were in the hands of fate and I hated it.

Lacing up my boots and working a shift with the dog I knew inside out would have brought me the calm I so desperately needed. I've always found a calm in the chaos of work and more than anything I wanted that feeling, but I had to be there for Claire and Ben and Eryn. Work would have to wait and I'd have to try to cope with and quieten the panic that kept threatening to overwhelm me.

The Tuesday morning after Eryn's second birthday we dropped her at Claire's parents and drove to the hospital. Ben's dad was meeting us there but, while I was taking a back seat, I wanted to be there for both Ben and Claire. I kissed Ben's head, said my goodbyes and made way for his parents, positioning myself at the back of the room.

Ben was prepped for the operation and the surgeon came to speak to him ahead of the anaesthetic. He asked if the surgeon would have to shave his head and the promise was made that no one would let that happen. I could see from the back of the room that his hair staying intact alleviated some of Ben's stress and couldn't help but smile at the thought of the young man he was turning into.

Ben was the bravest I've seen any child be. He's always been a stoic lad but he held it all in until he was wheeled through the doors to the operating theatre. Holding Claire's hand, he turned to her, crying, 'Mum, I don't want to die ...' She kissed his head and let the doors close before she broke down.

The surgery lasted seven and a half hours and Claire cried for the first hour but, once she'd calmed down, I decided to leave her and Ben's dad to it. I felt like Ben was my son but I knew he wasn't and I had to respect his dad's position. Besides, I didn't want to impose my worry on top of theirs so I spent the time Ben was under at the kennels with Theo. I told him what was going on, said sorry that he was stuck in kennels and fed him before making my way back to the hospital.

I'd been back at the hospital around an hour when the surgeon came and told us things had gone as well as expected. We were told things might take a while to settle down post-surgery, that Ben might temporarily not be able to speak, or know who we were, but it wouldn't last.

When he was wheeled onto the recovery ward, he had all his hair and was starting to come round. The surgeon who'd promised not to shave his hair had gently plucked what he needed to away so he could access the tumour. His entire head was iodine yellow, where they'd disinfected him before the surgery.

'Hi, Mum.'

Hearing Ben's voice and hearing him call Claire by her name was such a relief.

'Hiya, Gaz.'

'Alright, sunshine, you okay?'

Ben recovered well and was in hospital for two weeks. The brain tumour was cancerous – which they'd prepared us for – but they were confident they had all of it and he was put on medication. They'd discussed the fact he might need radiotherapy but wanted to start with medication first.

On 6 April 2013, I should have welcomed my bride walking down the aisle into matrimony and a happy ever after; instead I spent it on the moors with Theo. It might sound selfish but the feeling of being helpless for my kids made me want to hide. Searching for some peace, I needed to escape, to disappear, and I got that on the moors. A couple of days later, I went back to work. My bosses offered me more time off – I could have taken a week or two, but being on shift was my way of coping with everything. Working with Theo, I could relax and try to process what we'd been through. It was what I did best and I needed it to help me cope.

Claire didn't understand my desire to go back when I didn't have to. She worked for the same force so knew going back was my decision, not anyone else's, and it's something she found hard to understand. She'd been through enough so I chose not to offload on her, not to tell her how I felt I wasn't coping, that the fear of losing Eryn and then Ben in such quick succession had left a lasting impact on me. I wasn't sleeping, found concen-trating hard, I felt myself anger and snap when I should have been tender and understanding, but I knew I couldn't process what had happened without Theo.

I know how selfish that sounds but I worked in an environment where we controlled things. Where what we said went. Where we could make things okay for people and solve problems. I needed to feel I was still capable of that because, so far that year, I'd felt like I wasn't in control of anything. I'd nearly lost two of the things I loved the most and, while I knew Claire had too, she seemed to cope better emotionally than me. I felt helpless, like I should have been able to fix it, or should have seen it coming.

I'd replay the drive to football with Ben before it all happened, cursing myself for having taken Theo for a walk that day and not stayed and watched.

I blamed myself for not seeing any signs in Eryn.

Put bluntly, I felt like I'd messed up at home not being able to fix things so I selfishly wanted to get back to an environment where I could make a difference to help me process things. I longed to be useful; I needed Theo because he was the one who could restore me, the partner who knew exactly what I needed and could deliver it. As far as I was concerned, I was more than useless at home and hadn't been able to fix anything. At work, with Theo beside me, we could fix plenty between us.

As a couple and a family, we'd been to hell and back in the space of a few months, but Theo was my world too and while the wheels had been falling off the wagon at home, he had been sat in kennels waiting for me, not knowing what was going on, desperate to work again, waiting to jump back in the van with the lights going on the way to catch a baddie.

I felt a huge division of loyalty.

Theo was my family too and I felt like I'd let him down. He'd shown such promise in early jobs, then with Eryn and Ben both getting ill our progression had slowed and he had no idea why. I was determined together we'd be the best but with what had gone on at home our progress had pretty much halted.

With everything that had happened, Claire and I watched our relationship unravel and, because we were both in shock and trying to deal with what had happened, neither of us did anything to save it. During the period we were apart, I grew to rely on Theo more than ever: he was a life raft in a storm I was struggling to navigate through. I know now I should have clung to my fiancée, to our relationship; instead I was clinging to a dog. I knew everything Theo was thinking, but I knew nothing Claire thought. Or at least it seemed that way to me. We'd have the occasional argument where she would tell me I loved Theo more than her, that I cared more about him than her. It's tough to admit, but I honestly don't know if she was right or wrong. What I do know is back then, life with Theo was simple, everything with Claire seemed complex.

With Theo, I felt so alive every time we were on a chase. The closer we were to the edge of disaster, the calmer I felt. We'd turn up to jobs when all else had failed. When the trails had gone cold, when the suspects had been lost … We'd turn up and save the day.

Two heroes with six legs between us.

I should have invested more in my relationship with Claire, I know that now, but at a time when everything seemed so complex, being with Theo, catching the baddies and making our little corner of the world safer felt right, and for that reason I loved him more. Claire and I avoided each other as much as we could and lived in different rooms. She spent time at her parents' and because of my shift patterns it was easy to pass each other by, each of us watching our relationship unravel when we should have been celebrating being newlyweds.

9

With home life a mess, work became an even bigger focus. I was working nights in July 2013, when I was called to a job near home towards the end of our shift.

It was a massive track: there'd been a burglary, the suspect had run off when the police arrived and Theo had tracked for a few miles to get the suspect and ultimately detained him. For a job that looked like it was going nowhere, Theo had saved the day and caught the baddie again. I was elated but where I'd usually tell Claire, our communication was far from where it should have been.

We were existing in the same house, the same space, but not as close as we'd once been. I should have just been honest and told her how much I loved her, missed her, needed her, but I was an idiot. Instead I let my stubborn and arrogant streak take over so I kept quiet.

The next week we were called to another burglary. The thieves were still there so time was of the essence. By the time we got there, they'd made off, but we began the search. There was a lot of noise and activity, a squad car was there and I knew for us to have the best shot Theo needed peace. I asked everyone to leave and they did as I asked.

'You okay, Theo? Do you reckon you can find it? Come on, let's go for a walk!'

It was a trick I'd learned from my dog-handling partner Andy Beaver when we were first paired with him when we passed out. I knew Theo felt pressure when we turned up to a busy job with expectation on what he could do and I'd seen Andy's dog Milo feel the same thing. It was like he could sense the expectation and it stressed him. Andy would take him out of the fray and walk him a bit to get him to calm down and relax. When we can clear out a scene I can give Theo free rein, watch his body language more and give him his own headspace.

I trusted him but it's always easier to trust your dog when there's no one there. If eyewitnesses or cops first on the scene say they're sure a suspect went off one way and your dog is telling you another, it's easy to think you should side with what's been seen but the reality is that you should trust what your dog is telling you.

We got down to the bottom of the estate where I'd hoped Theo would pick up a scent and his entire body language changed. I knew he had something. Within seconds, he'd disappeared down the side of a house. I heard growls followed by a bite and I knew he'd been successful.

Not all handlers will say this and it's no slight at all on their training, but I knew Theo wouldn't just bite anyone. He senses adrenaline – it's a learned scent, but criminals being chased all give off adrenaline – so I knew he'd never nip someone out in their garden, having a fag. He's never ever bitten anyone he's not meant to, except me. I trusted him not to cock up and he never let me down.

It was the first job he'd taken the lead on and it was as though he was telling me that he knew my head was all over the place but he'd look after us at work while I got things in order. He'd found the suspect in a completely different area to the one we were told to search, but using his initiative, in the quiet of the night, he'd sorted it.

I started to feel like I was living for work. It was addictive: I'd been useless at home, but I could help people at work, I was useful. The more use I was to people, the more use I wanted to be. It was like an addiction.

I got home and Claire asked me how the shift had gone. It was the first time we'd talked properly in weeks and I was so proud of Theo. I told her about the job, every last detail of how well he'd done. We started reminiscing about Theo, which moved on to other things and the kids, and the next morning Claire gave me a letter telling me how much she loved me and how much we had going for us. It was the green light I needed and I told her I was determined we'd get back to where we'd been before the kids got sick. I knew that I wanted to marry her still, and within a couple of days the wedding was being planned again. Claire had done such a great job of organising it that our wedding planner had said when we cancelled it that all he needed was the okay and he could get us another date. We set a date for 28 September and it felt like everything was starting to fall back into place.

Two days before I'd say 'I do' to the woman of my dreams, Theo suffered what was his worst injury to date. He had a bad habit of spinning in the van and catching his tail in the metal grate. He'd done it loads and had cut or split his tail several times already. It's called 'happy tail syndrome' but every time it healed, he'd do it more and it'd get worse.

On 26 September, Theo had to have his tail amputated after splitting it again in the van. It could have been patched up again but he'd done it so frequently, it was just a matter of time before it needed to be amputated so I made the tough decision to get it done. It didn't change his life or the way he performed at work, but he'd always had such a beautiful, full tail. Now he'd have a stump. Claire and I were going away on honeymoon to Tenerife so I made the tough decision to get Theo's tail removed so he could rest up and be healed by the time I was back and we could get back to work. I was gutted and gave him a telling-off for being so daft before taking him into the vets.

It's not a straightforward operation: dogs' tails are part of their spine so there's a lot that can go wrong. Thankfully, everything went to plan and he was back and recovering the same day.

Claire and I were married on 28 September 2013. Ben, who was recovering well (and has thankfully remained clear after a year of recovery), was pageboy with his cousins. Eryn was a flower girl. It was perfect. P!nk's 'True Love' was our first dance. It's not a traditional first dance song, but it's always fitted us perfectly. Our love was never straightforward, nor was our relationship, so neither of us wanted our first dance to be like that either.

I said my vows meaning every word. I loved Claire with everything I had, but while the day was perfect from the outside looking in, a big part of me felt I didn't deserve it. I ignored it, I pushed it aside, I drank beer to get it out of my head, but while I was so utterly in love with her, I couldn't shake a nagging doubt.

I'd always known Claire was beautiful, plenty of mates ribbed me, constantly telling me I was punching above my weight. I could see it in the looks of strangers when we were out together. I'm no oil painting, Claire is. Our temporary separation had left me questioning a lot and while I was delighted we were back together and getting married, I had a negative feeling I couldn't shake. Maybe I should have asked her how she felt, told her I felt insecure, but I loved her and she'd said the same vows as me.

I ignored that feeling and entered married life hoping my love for her would be enough for both of us.

We took her mum and dad on honeymoon with us to Tenerife so they could be babysitters while we spent quality time together and, despite my doubts on the day, we had the best two weeks together.

I'd call work from Spain to check in with the kennel staff every day, making sure Theo was recovering okay. I begged them to be careful he didn't split his tail again or do anything that would slow his recovery. When we got back, I would be desperate to hit the ground running.

Claire would laugh at me checking in on him every day but I felt like I had a new purpose and I did a really good job of putting the feelings I'd felt on our wedding day behind me. I was married, I was a husband as well as a dad now, the whole tumultuousness of the last six months could be put behind us, things had fallen into order at home and I knew they were good at work too.

Everything seemed exactly where it should be.

Theo recovered and got back to work without a hitch, Eryn was better, Claire and I were saving to buy our first house; what had started out as potentially the worst year of my life had ended up with Eryn well again, a beautiful wife I adored and a dog who was getting better and stronger every single shift. But while the feelings I'd had on the wedding day quietened on our honeymoon, they were never truly far from my thoughts once we got back.

Claire was beautiful, so jaw-droppingly beautiful I'd wonder why she was with me sometimes. I knew I was the best at work, I knew I was a good handler and that Theo was an amazing police dog, but at home I kept feeling like I was never good enough for my wife.

Eryn and Ben adored me and I knew I was a good dad and stepdad, but there was always a part of Claire I felt like I couldn't reach, a part she kept away from me, and

I'd blame myself: if I was everything to her, she wouldn't need to keep a bit of herself back.

It was my fault for not being enough for her, I reasoned. I'd try and bring it up sometimes but there's not much you can say when you feel that way which doesn't make you sound like you're an insecure mess and very unattractive.

Besides, Claire had been through so much with Eryn too, I didn't want to put her through anything else. I didn't want the way I felt – my problems, my issue – to become hers. I'd also played through a scenario in my head where I'd tell her how I'd felt on our wedding day and ask her if she really loved me, if she really wanted to be with me. While in the make-believe scenario I hoped she'd tell me she loved me, there was a very real chance she could say the opposite. I loved her so much, though, I was scared to ask that and lose everything. I'd spend hours walking Theo, wondering whether I was just an insecure idiot who was overthinking things or I should trust my intuition. I can't have been easy to live with at that point, I know that.

Despite my feelings, during our first Christmas as a married couple there was a lot to be thankful for.

I worked up until the holiday and we made the most of being in our home for a final Christmas. We'd decided in November to move in with Claire's mum and dad in 2014 so we could save for a house and get on the property ladder sooner rather than later. They had plenty of space for us, and while it might sound like the death knell for many relationships, for us it was the start of the happiest eighteen months of our marriage. There was no hassle – Claire's mum did everything for us so we could spend quality time together and with the kids. Claire was never bored or on her own so if I got back from a shift and wanted to escape for a long walk with Theo to process jobs, I could.

Claire's dad had been a handler for twenty-six years so we had loads in common. I'd finish a shift and he and I would sit with a glass of red, reminiscing about jobs.

In addition to being with Theo as much as I wanted, Claire could do what she wanted too and we had babysitters on tap if we wanted to go out together. We had our own lounge, our own bedrooms for us and the kids. It was as close to perfect as married life gets.

Claire and I had always worked opposite shifts when we were renting because one of us had to be home with the children, but with her parents around we could work the same shifts, which gave us more time together, both at work and out of it. We worked out of stations close to each other so Claire would see me working too. I'd patrol around her area purposely when I knew she was working nights – I wanted to make sure her area was as safe as it could be while she was policing it. She'd know about jobs from colleagues and be the first to see when we did something good.

In November that year, Theo and I were flying and life was good. I loved being on shift with Claire. As shifts go, it was a pretty regular one, but towards the end we got a shout for a 'Thieves on!' – there was a team trying to break into premises in Oldham.

It was an industrial estate and those tracks can be tough because they're so vast and there can be a lot of tracking back on yourself. There's no straight path or route through and a chance on such a vast scale that whoever is hiding can change location several times and an area your dog has discounted could suddenly have a scent on it the second time around. Basically, they can be a pain in the backside.

I set Theo up at the entrance. There were plenty of police cars there and I knew Claire was listening on the radio because she was on shift at another job. I issued the challenges and sent Theo in. He started searching as he normally did, but without warning he suddenly flew in a different direction heading without a second thought over a five-foot concrete wall. I saw him clear it with his usual effortlessness but, where I'd normally follow without a second thought, something stopped me from jumping over it.

I ran and looked over and there was a fifteen-foot drop on the other side of it. There was razor wire all along the drop and stuck, hanging, was Theo, suspended in razor wire, blood already seeping from where he'd been cut. I could see a mix of blood and mud on the floor where his weight had hit the deck but then he'd been pulled back up and he was stuck, with the razor wire in him.

First, Eryn, then Ben, now Theo, my third child.

I knew if he moved and started to try to free himself or pull himself around, he'd be dead. The razor wire was inside his back legs and thighs and his front legs were anchored in wire too. He was losing blood and I knew if he struggled he could die. His blood pressure was already high because he'd been in a chase and was pumping blood fast.

I screamed at him to stay still and, miraculously, he did exactly as he was told, like he knew things were very serious. Then I shouted on the radio, 'The dog's been impaled!' I heard Claire scream down the radio, 'What's going on with Theo?'

A patrol car turned up to help and, within seconds, colleagues as panicked as we were surrounded us. Everyone in the entire Greater Manchester Police loves the dogs so when one is hurt if anyone can help they will. A couple of sets of pliers appeared from nowhere and I remember suspending Theo to make sure his weight wasn't on the razor wires while he was gently cut free, still bleeding. He was panicked and I could see it in his big brown eyes but while they implored me to make it all better, all I could do was hold his weight, keep him still and try and soothe his nerves with some gentle words: 'You're alright, son. Don't worry, mate, we'll get you sorted in a second. What were you thinking, you big, daft sod? Keep still, good lad.'

I never took my eyes off him, not even for a second. He kept eye contact with me the whole time too; he knew not to move or he could make it worse. Maintaining eye contact with him would keep him calm, I knew. Theo normally knew what to do in any situation, but this time he was utterly clueless. He'd never seen razor wire before, had never been hurt this badly before, never been suspended before or unable to get free. He was in pain and I could tell his adrenaline was pumping.

As the guys from the patrol cars cut the wire, I peeled it away, keeping eye contact with him, and let my hands stroke him to find the injuries. He had cuts that were deep, but for a second I thought it wasn't anywhere near as bad as I'd suspected it was going to be. Once free of the wire, holding his weight still until I could make sure he was okay, I carried him to the van and set him down in the back. He was exhausted and scared and I could tell how glad he was to be back in familiar surroundings.

I started washing him down and checking every inch of him. His fur is very thick so it's a meticulous job to make sure he hasn't cut deep. He stood up gently and I ran my hands between his front legs to stroke him and my fingers disappeared inside him. I felt sick to the core and he locked eyes with me, reading my expression and realising it was serious.

He'd severed his leg under his chest, where his armpit was.

So I rushed him to the emergency vet, calling ahead to let them know what had happened and how serious it was. I managed to call Claire before we arrived and fill her in. She made me promise to call the second I had any news.

When we arrived, Theo was ushered in and I was told to leave him there, they'd call once they'd stitched him up. Every dog owner will know when you take your dog to the vet for an operation you always have to sign a form that says you won't blame them if your beloved animal doesn't wake up. I felt sick signing it, but hugged Theo and kissed his head. I told him I loved him and I'd see him soon. As I drove home afterwards, it was getting light out.

I've always hated dropping Theo at the vets but this was the worst. I felt like I'd abandoned him. I knew he was in safe hands but the fact of the matter was that we'd started the shift as a partnership, entered the vets together and now I was leaving him. It was like I was leaving my child at the side of the road and driving away. I felt instantly empty without him but that emptiness was paired with an overwhelmingly deep chasm of fear and worry about what might happen to him. I felt sick and I felt hollow.

Despite trying to sleep, it wouldn't come. I still had adrenaline in my system and replayed everything. Could I have done anything different? Should I have kept him on a lead? Should I have noticed the incision sooner? I knew it wasn't my fault but I knew it had happened because of me and maybe if I'd done something different, Theo would be out in his kennel and I'd be fast asleep.

By 10 a.m. the next day, I couldn't wait any longer and called the vet to see how he was doing. They told me he hadn't come round yet but they'd found more than the initial wound and they'd had to shave him. I headed straight down there and he was cut to ribbons. His thick fur had done its usual job of concealing what was going on underneath. He had twelve stitches in his front leg, seven in his flank, four inside his thigh, there were nicks and cuts where they couldn't stitch him, but because he'd hit the deck before being suspended, he'd bruised his entire leg and haemorrhaged his muscle. Where they'd shaved him to stitch him, he was black all over his entire leg, with deep, painful-looking bruising.

I was shocked by what I saw – I didn't consider that dogs could bruise but it was huge. The type of bruise that if you'd seen it on a human, you'd wince.

He was off for four weeks while he recuperated. I made sure he didn't move too much, that he didn't bother his stitches. Every day, I spent hours with him in his kennel, making sure he didn't try and do too much too soon and keeping him company while he recovered.

Claire knew how worried I was; she understood because of what she'd seen her dad go through. So when she suggested a weekend away in the Lake District the week before Theo went back on duty, I agreed.

I put Theo into the work kennels for a week of rest and relaxation and I knew he'd be taken care of and made a fuss of. The other handlers had been calling constantly to see how he was doing and I knew they'd be happy to have the hero of the hour back. It was a relaxing weekend but I thought about Theo constantly – I couldn't wait to get back to work and check he was okay. More than anything, though, I couldn't wait to get back on duty and do what we did best.

One of the other handlers brought him back to me in her van within half an hour of us arriving home. I don't know who was more excited, him or me. He spun in the van to bark at Sinead's dog and say goodbye, but as Theo spun, he caught his foot on the boot cap – a little piece of metal. He sliced his toe and blood started pouring. I thanked Sinead and took him straight into the garden so I could check how bad it was. While I knew his stitches were fully recovered and his toe wasn't serious, I realised straight away it would keep us off duty until it was recovered.

It was the straw that broke the camel's back and I had a huge go at him in the garden, like he was a petulant child: 'You're kidding me, Theo! Honestly, you've got to be having a laugh. I've only just got you back, you've only just recovered and now this, because you're daft? I've got to go back to that bloody vet now, look at the state of you!' It wasn't his fault, but I was so frustrated with him: we were supposed to be brand new and back at work, but thanks so his excitement and clumsiness, we'd be benched for a while longer.

I took him straight back to the vet and explained what had happened. The vet examined him and determined it was a pretty bad cut – there was a chance Theo might lose his toe as a result of his giddiness. I'd thought he'd be patched up and we'd be back in a few days so the idea that he might lose his toe sent me into a tailspin. He was off for another fortnight but managed to keep his toe.

The next two weeks were an absolute pain in the backside for me, though. If I'm benched, Theo stays in kennels because he's my dog and no one else can work him. But if he's benched, I turn into a skivvy. I was driving people around, helping train other dogs, working in the kennels, trying to gently rehab Theo with walks and lead work. It was beyond frustrating for both of us.

Theo would look at me sheepishly every morning, fully aware his behaviour meant we were both sidelined for another couple of weeks but, as always, I couldn't stay mad with him. His eyes are such a window into his soul, they always have been. He's transparent when you look into those huge brown eyes. He can't hide his excitement and he can't hide it when he feels guilty too.

10

WE WERE FINALLY BACK ON SHIFT at 100 per cent fitness in the middle of December 2014.

Theo was hungry to work and I couldn't wait to get back out there either. Before our first shift, I gave him a pep talk, warning him not to get injured again or he'd have to buy the vet a pint himself. We eased back in with the regular jobs we'd been used to and Theo was back like he'd never been away. His tracking and bites were exactly what they'd been before his lengthy spell of injury and the worries I'd had about him deskilling while he recovered never materialised.

We were on nights the week before Christmas and a burglary came in around 3 a.m. in the middle of our shift. Items had been taken from the house and they'd stolen the car on the drive too. It was round the corner from where I used to live so I knew the area well. When the call came across the radio I was letting Theo have a wee on a local field nearby. He's always known when I'm excited by the pitch in my voice and when I started telling him to hurry up and come on, his stump of a tail got going.

We ran back to the van, I pulled out the car park and we were on our way. I kept thinking I knew the area well and that it could be a nice job, that we should be able to get them fairly easily. We were almost there with the lights on when a red car came absolutely screaming past, going around 90mph in a 30 zone. We were only a couple of miles away and it was the middle of the night. It matched the description of the vehicle we'd been given over the radio and I was positive this was the car we were looking for.

We weren't the first to spot it and, seconds later, a police car zoomed by. We joined the pursuit and saw the driver abandon the car and make off in an alleyway between rows of terraced houses. I sent Theo and we managed to get him in a garden. I issued the challenges and he gave up so Theo didn't bite. He barked until I got there and I called him off. Division came as backup and arrested him.

I took Theo back to the van for a drink, but as we passed the abandoned vehicle I saw it was filled with presents – wrapped Christmas presents. The scumbag had broken into someone's house and nicked all their Christmas presents. You could tell by the wrapping the majority of them were destined for kids.

It was the worst scenario to come across just a few days before Christmas. The usual procedure would be to evidence it all and take it away but I knew if we did that, some kids in Manchester would be waking up on Christmas Day with nothing to open. I went out on a limb and took photographs of everything in situ, logging every detail I could. I'd put in my statement that I'd found it and cleared the decision up the line that we'd try and reunite the presents with their owners. The thought of a child waking up on Christmas morning, having had all their presents stolen, was too much.

I put all the gifts in the van and went to the address we'd been given when the call came through. It was around 4 a.m. and all we could do was wander up and down the road, looking for signs of forced entry. Theo eventually found a house where a side door had been kicked in.

I knocked as quietly as I could, the window upstairs was opened and a bloke called down, asking what I wanted. I said I was a policeman and could he come down and open the door.

There's something about being a police officer: every single time you knock on a door on a night shift after midnight, no one will ever answer the front door. Whoever you're knocking will always come to the bedroom window, open it and ask what you want. You get accustomed to it so I did my usual and knocked on the door before taking a couple of steps back and looking up at the window.

After gently explaining he'd been broken into, he and his wife (who'd come down in her dressing gown) were distraught. They hadn't heard a thing but the back door needed to be replaced, the presents from under the tree and under the stairs had gone, the car was gone, the house had been ransacked and they were understandably heartbroken. It was such a horrible feeling for them, they were beside themselves. Their two kids were asleep upstairs but I reassured them we had all their gifts and everything was recovered. I helped them patch up the back door until the morning and put all the presents back under the tree.

They made me a cuppa and gave Theo a fuss. By the time we got back to the van, both of us were grinning.

'Theo, you've just saved Christmas,' I told him.

It remains to this day one of the best jobs we've ever done. Theo was just doing what he knew. For him it was

A special bond: relaxing with Eryn after his swim (left); a typical walk with Eryn, in her romper suit (centre left); Eryn helping to clean the kennels, and Theo being super gentle, as usual (bottom left).

Above: Even though Theo had power, he was so, so gentle on the lead with Eryn.

By the trig point
the moors, with
Theo, Wentwort
(pug) and Kiera
(Theo's sister).
We'd often come
here to walk and
unwind.

This was supposed to be
my wedding day, 6 April
2013, but I went to the
moors with Theo, after
Ben's operation, to take
stock of everything.

Theo's amputated tail! He stayed inside that night and slept by me in the kitchen, which is an important part of the healing process for injured dogs and their handlers!

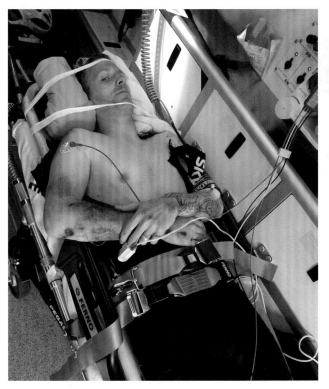

...he ambulance after I ...shed my pedal bike ...2mph and destroyed ...shoulder and collar ...e.

How I always remember night-shift duty – with Theo alert and ready by my side.

Theo could show his serious side when needed.

Training Kai on heel work. I taught him from scratch.

Theo is a hard act to follow. 'Ginger Giant' Kai, a Malinois, has been accepted by Theo and is becoming a fantastic successor (left); Mako couldn't quite cut it as a police dog, but he'll be a great pet (below and bottom left).

Being licked by Sevvy after learning he would be taken off me. I was so upset, but this just sums up the little man – always ready for some fuss and love!

Theo and Sevvy side by side for the last time at work.

Special moments together: on top of the trig point on the moors (above); when I was in a low mood, Theo simply came over and rested his head on mine as if to offer support (left).

Those incredible eyes.

a day, a shift, a job like any other. He'll never know the difference he made to that family.

From the start of 2014 Theo had grown daily in strength and confidence. Little by little, he was becoming more my equal and less my police dog. It started slowly when he'd come through the hatch in the van and sit up the front with me. After a few too many times of him staring at me while I ate my cheese sandwich on shift after a job, he'd get half if he'd done a good track or assisted an arrest.

Every morning, he would greet me like every dog does. Whether I hadn't seen him for ten minutes or ten hours, the adoration was there, the stump of his tail would go and no matter what sort of mood I was in or how tired I was, just seeing his eagerness and excitement never failed to put a smile on my face and lift my spirits. I adored every bone in his body – getting to work with him every single day was like every boyhood dream I'd had about being a handler come true. He was a better police dog than I'd ever dared dream of having and we got each other like the most successful of human police partners do.

I'd spend hours sitting with him in his kennel when we were off shift, chatting to him, stroking him. He became my greatest confidant, the only one I truly trusted, who I felt really knew me. At work, I relied on him to keep me safe and to help me do the job I loved, but I relied on him away from the force too – no one knew me like he did. I wouldn't even have to say anything and he'd know what I was thinking by my body language. It was like he'd sense if I was thinking about taking him for a walk or cleaning out his kennel at home, he was completely in tune with me.

Theo and Eryn were growing closer too – he adored her and it was like he knew she was the smallest and most vulnerable member of our pack. They'd play the peg bag game in the garden, my daughter giggling with delight as he trailed round after her. I'd marvel at the fact that a creature so ferocious at work could be so tender and loving at home. Eryn would help me with the kennel at home and Theo would be so gentle with her, he'd keep his strength and size under control around her and he adored her.

Christmas that year was perfect: Claire's mum and dad cooked up a storm, the kids loved having their grandparents fuss over them so much on the big day and Theo had his Christmas dinner in a bowl outside with some nice warm gravy while we enjoyed ours in the house.

The year 2015 started as perfectly as 2014 had ended. I loved home and Claire and I were house hunting – we'd stayed with her parents over a year and knew at some point we'd have to step off what felt like a perpetual holiday, become grown-ups and move into our own place with the kids. Meanwhile, work was brilliant too. As I've said, I loved helping people and feeling needed.

Claire and I took the kids on holiday in January 2015. We had an amazing time in Tenerife, but I hated being away from Theo and she sensed it. There'd been a tiny shift in us as a married couple. I was obsessed with work and I know I was. It meant everything to me, it defined me and gave me a great sense of pride. I'd have been a dog handler for free so getting paid for it, having it as my job and that job affording us a house was something else, but the dedication I had to work meant there was less space in my head and heart for my marriage. It also meant that when I couldn't work, because Theo was injured or we were on holiday, I wasn't as relaxed as I should have been. I needed work to feel at peace, it was a huge part of who I was. I was Gareth the Greater Manchester Police dog handler and, yes, I was a husband and a father too, but my job gave me a sense of purpose – it defined me, maybe more than it should have done. Theo was like my left hand and because he needed me to care for him, walk him, clean his kennel, even when I wasn't working, he took up a lot of my time.

We had a fantastic holiday and spent amazing quality time with the children, but – as always – it was a relief to get back on the job with my best mate. A few days after we returned, I was just coming off a night shift. Claire was working the day and I knew we'd cross over. It had been a busy shift, I was in the van and was back at the unit at 5.10 a.m. I finished at 7 a.m. and would be back in time to get the kids to school; I knew Claire would be leaving the house around 5.15 a.m.

I was about to start cleaning out the van when the text alarm went off on my phone: it was from Claire and just said 'Help'. I started to reply when she phoned me and all I could hear was screaming. She was screaming like I'd never heard her scream before. Like I'd never heard anyone scream before.

As a police officer, I see trauma all the time – I hear it, I deal with it. I see death, grief, violence. None of it fazes me, nothing gets to me or bothers me. Of course, I feel a sadness for whoever is left behind and on long walks and downtime I process things, but I can cope with it – if I couldn't, I might just as well hand in my warrant card. It's my job and I deal with it because I have Theo beside me.

But to hear Claire screaming and crying down the phone – the bottom dropped out of my world. But I didn't get a chance to say anything before she shouted out the registration of a car. I recognised the registration and felt my stomach lurch. It had been doing jobs all night and we'd missed it, trying to ram people off the roads, thefts, carjackings. We'd always been too late to the scene so I knew the instant I heard the registration, Claire had been a victim of a carjacking.

'What's going on, Claire? CLAIRE?'

I couldn't contain my rising panic. I could hear a commotion on the phone but I had no idea where she was and I was powerless to stop what was happening to her. Through tears and screams, she replied, 'Gaz, he's hit me. He's hit me. Gaz, help …'

I could hear her screaming and then the phone went dead. As a police officer, you can process that sound, that panic quickly and deal with it, but as a husband I was absolutely terrified.

Theo was already out the van and in my car, ready to go home. He was dozing, having worked a long shift, but I knew I needed him to bring his A game – this was to be the biggest job of our lives.

I shouted up on the divisional radio with my call sign, '6143, urgent!' When you say that word, everyone knows you're in trouble or you know about some trouble so everyone listens and everyone mobilises.

'My wife's off-duty, she's on her way to work ... I think she's getting carjacked ... Send a patrol, she's somewhere on this route!'

There was a six-mile stretch of roads she could have been on – a huge area to cover. I jumped in the van and switched on my radio, telling all vehicles I was en route. Meanwhile, Theo could sense something wasn't right: we weren't doing what we normally did at the end of a shift and I have no doubt he could sense the chemical changes in me with the stress hormones and adrenaline I felt coursing through me and making me physically shake as I drove that van faster than I'd ever driven it before.

I didn't know it at the time but there was a discussion going on in the operations room to stop me going. Claire was family, so technically speaking I shouldn't have attended, but the head in the operations room knew better than to call me off the job.

Nothing. Not a single thing on God's earth was going to stop me getting to my wife and making her safe. I might not have been carrying a firearm but I had a weapon in Theo and my bosses were scared I'd use it. I was Claire's husband and she's the mother of my children. I could have found her dead or dying on the side of the road and taken matters into my own hands. What they didn't know, though, was that while I loved my wife with everything I had I loved Theo and my job just as much. I'd do this job right and I wouldn't for one second jeopardise the job and the dog I loved by letting temper or anger get the better of me.

I got onto the road I suspected she was on. It's a straight road and I was flat out to get to her. I was scanning the road when a call came over the radio from a friend I worked with, who was in a patrol vehicle. He was behind the car being driven by the man who had attacked Claire and asking for assistance. If the car wasn't with Claire anymore, the assault must have stopped. I quickly reasoned there was nothing I could physically do to help her now: a patrol car had just arrived with her, an ambulance was on its way – she was in the best hands possible. What Theo and I could do, though, was find the car and catch the men who'd done this to her.

I asked the patrol car how she was. They replied saying she was okay but had been punched and assaulted. She was in shock and needed some medical attention but there was nothing life-threatening.

I swung the car around and went in the direction of the patrol car chasing the driver of the vehicle who'd hurt Claire. Knowing she was safe, autopilot went on. I switched into work mode and knew I had to do what we did best.

Both Theo and I were on a heightened sense of awareness.

The patrol car lost the vehicle in Lees but soon found it again, abandoned with the doors open. Whoever had driven it was nowhere to be seen. The patrol car knew I was on my way and they knew Theo had the best nose in the force. If anyone stood a chance of catching who'd done this to Claire, it was Theo and me.

'Don't get out your van!'

Using my radio, I requested any officers that arrived on the scene to stay in their vehicles and not get out and examine the abandoned car. I didn't want the scene contaminated with other scents. Theo would get this done, I knew, but I wanted to make it as easy for him as possible. It wasn't even light yet so I knew there wouldn't be many people about. The offender's scent pattern would be the strongest and freshest one and Theo would be able to lock on and do his job.

I pulled up a couple of minutes later. My head was in gear and I knew I'd do it right. I spoke to the patrol car, who said no one had been out of their vehicles. There were terraced houses on either side of the road; it was a suburban search. Every few houses there was an alleyway and the car had been abandoned right by one of those alleyways.

I knew he'd gone down there, but as a dog handler the worst thing you can do is presume you know more than a dog's nose. Dogs have 300 million olfactory or scent receptors in their noses compared with 6 million for us humans. Not only do they sense smell better, they process it better too. The part of their brain that analyses smell and can follow a trail is, comparatively speaking, forty times bigger than the same area in our brain. I trusted Theo's nose with my life and now I trusted him to help my wife.

Normally on a rush job, where time is of the essence, I get Theo out the front. He comes through the hatch and out the driver's side door. This time, though, I went round to the back of the van – I needed him to know how much this job meant, what was at stake.

'Theo, listen to me, son. If you're ever going to prove to me you're the dog that I want and need, I need you to find him for me. I need you to. You can be the worst police dog for the rest of your career, but I need you to find him. You have to, son. You have to!'

I wanted to show Claire I was the man who could protect her, that I could keep her safe.

Theo looked at me with the same look he'd given me on the very first day we met. He got what I needed and he knew how much I needed it.

'Please, please find him ...'

I didn't even issue a search command, I released Theo and asked, 'Where is he?' And he took off. He sniffed the car and round it a bit, his nose hit the ground and he was off down the alleyway. He jumped two fences and was about to jump a third when he froze – I didn't even have a chance to catch up with him when he turned and disappeared behind a shed. I was sure he'd found him. Theo wouldn't bite unless this guy tried to run off, I knew, so I was sure he had him penned in. When I caught up, the guy wasn't there. There was evidence he'd been resting there and had taken off again.

When a police car is chasing you, the adrenaline starts going. It'll carry you over a few fences and through a few gardens at a pretty fast sprint, but at some point it'll wear off. Quite often on searches like this you find somewhere the assailant has been resting before you actually find them.

The man who'd beaten my wife had run out of puff less than half a mile from where he'd ditched the car.

He'd hidden, caught his breath, calmed down a bit and was on the run again, leaving money and the car keys on the floor.

Theo lay down, which indicated he was pleased with his find. It was a start but not enough: I needed to find the man. I praised him briefly, then pushed him on. All the while I could hear more and more police cars arriving and so I shouted on the radio, 'No one get out! If you get out, you'll mess it up. I need it to be sterile!' I knew Theo needed the best chance he had, not a scene contaminated with other dogs searching too. If he lost the track, I'd have to take him back to the car to recapture the scent and start all over again.

A fellow handler replied on the radio that they were going to do a perimeter search of the estate and some cars would drive round to let him know we were there. In situations like this when criminals know they're surrounded or there's a lot of manpower looking for them, quite often they go to ground. They'll stay put, find somewhere to hide in the hope they can wait it out and make their escape when we've all given up.

While Theo searched, I needed this guy to hear the cars and know there were plenty of people looking for him. I switched my radio dial down so Theo could focus

– I'd have stayed all week to find this man and I knew I wasn't about to give up. Now getting lighter, dawn was on its way. It was a freezing morning, but I didn't feel anything.

After searching for around fifteen minutes, Theo and I met a female PC doing a perimeter check. She told me she hadn't gone any further than where she was standing and Theo indicated there was nothing that way anyway. One of tons of possibilities shut off and I knew, little by little, we'd narrow the search field until we had him, the man who had beaten and terrified my wife.

Theo started in a new direction. There was frost on a wall and he cleared it in seconds. It was an unusual route for him to take, a split-level wall in between two houses. I knew he was onto something because it wasn't where anyone would have gone naturally, but I followed and saw him a few feet in front of me turn to the left.

Seeing Theo or any police dog get a scent is something really magical to observe. It's like Theo hoovers when he thinks he's onto something – he'll inhale as much of the scent as he can so it stays set in his brain. If he's only got a little bit of it, he could get distracted or confuse it for something else. When he's hoovered it up, it's like he has it set in his mind and won't confuse it for anything else.

He hoovered the bottom of a fence and I knew he'd found him.

I'll never forget how Theo took an almighty breath in and I could see his chest cavity expand. He exhaled the biggest breath I've ever seen him exhale, like a dragon breathing out smoke as the warm air from his lungs hit the freezing atmosphere. I crept over to where he was and looked over the fence. I couldn't see anything, but we both went over.

Theo ran across the garden on the other side and I heard all hell break loose behind some bushes. I was in the moment in the middle of the job but it was the proudest I've ever been of him: Theo had a hold of his ankle but he was a big lad and was putting up a fight. Between the two of us we managed to subdue him as the police patrols who'd been looking too caught up with us.

I took a second to whisper that I loved him before I put Theo back on his lead as the lad in question was arrested. Theo had done such a great job of detaining him – he'd been measured, but ferocious enough to let this lad know he meant business. When arrested, the lad asked to be put in the van. He wanted to get away from the pair of us who'd caught him.

'I'm sorry, boss, I didn't know she was a girl ...' His pathetic excuse trailed off.

'That wasn't just a girl, that was my wife and the mother of my children,' I said. Of course I shouldn't have told him but I wanted him to know.

After asking a policeman present to take him away, I walked Theo back to the van. I sat on the floor with Theo and he sat in front of me.

'Thank you so much, son. Thank you. I can't ever repay you enough … You are the best. It doesn't matter what you do now, I'll never, ever forget tonight. For the rest of my life, I'll never forget what you did for me and for us tonight.'

Throughout the rest of Theo's career and out of all the arrests he's made, that's the one that meant the most to me. The one I'll never be able to repay him for.

Relief flooded through me that we'd caught the guy who'd hurt my wife and I'd managed to keep my temper in check. The old Gareth would have knocked seven bells out of him, but I'd handled it exactly as I should. If it wasn't for Theo, I might have behaved differently, but I knew if I did then I'd have lost my job on the Dog Unit, lost Theo and been back to square one.

Theo had been Claire's saviour that night, but the love I had for him saved my job too. I promised myself and him I'd never let him down and if I'd let temper get the better of me, I'd have done just that.

I phoned Claire's mum to speak to Claire and she was upset but okay: 'Thank you so much, Gaz ...' She trailed off, crying.

I told her I'd be home soon.

11

I GOT THEO BACK TO HOUGH END and put him in a kennel while I cleaned down the van. I was trying to process it all but the enormity of what he'd done kept washing over my mind and overwhelming me. A job that should have taken ten minutes took double the time because I kept going back to give him a fuss and say thank you for what he'd just achieved. A fellow handler offered to finish the cleaning up for me but I needed something mundane to help get my head together before I went home.

After I sorted the van, I washed Theo down and put him in my car for the journey home. When I got home, there were officers taking pictures of Claire's injuries and collecting her clothes for forensics. Claire hates a fuss being made of her and she doesn't like being the centre of attention so while I could tell she was uncomfortable with it all, I gave her a big hug and put Theo in the garden.

It was only 10 a.m. and I was exhausted.

Claire came out into the garden and she and Theo had a moment together. Understandably, she wanted to thank him herself, and as she did so I got his breakfast ready. I'd made him some gravy to warm his belly up – it had been a cold morning and I wanted him to have an extra treat anyway. I could have sat in the kennels with him all day, thanking him. He had no idea he'd done anything extraordinary, though – I could see he was confused by the fuss and the attention. He meant more to me at that moment than anything because he'd helped keep the family I loved together. To him it was just another job and we'd done what we were supposed to do, what we'd done hundreds of times before. But it was more than that, way more. I desperately wanted him to understand, but knew he never would.

After colleagues questioned the suspect and took statements from Claire, the events of that night unfolded. She had been on her way to work when a car had pulled out across the road in front of her. She'd beeped her horn and he'd done a U turn and started driving right behind her. When she'd stopped at lights, he'd attacked her.

Claire doesn't scare easily. She got out of the car to confront the reckless driver, but the lad – who wasn't small – had got out at the same time. Realising she was in trouble, Claire tried to get back in her car but hadn't made it in time before he'd grabbed the door and dragged her out.

Claire's 5ft 9in and was wearing a baseball cap with her hair tucked in it. The assailant had presumed she was a bloke and thumped her. He'd hit her hard and square in the face. I'd taken a punch from him so I knew he was strong; it must have terrified Claire. He'd hit her again before Claire managed to scramble back into her car and put the central locking on. He spent a few seconds trying to get into the car and then made off.

Claire wasn't left with any lasting injuries – there was swelling and bruising to her face and jaw but she was massively shaken up. The force of a punch to the face is something to be reckoned with and it had scared her a lot. We were both devastated, confused, angry and upset. I'd vowed to protect her when we married and she'd been punched, hard in the face, when I was nowhere near to help her.

That was the night I felt Theo the Legend was born. He's become a legendary force among handlers in the

Greater Manchester Police but from that night on he proved he had every right to the label.

I went to bed and by the time I woke up Claire was done with having people fuss over her – she wanted to get back to normal. She had a couple of days off to recover and I was back at work that night.

Eryn was four and so proud of Theo when I told her a very watered-down version of what had happened. She fussed him and cuddled him even more than usual and kept calling him our hero.

It took a while for me to process what had happened. I was back in the game and focused on work but it felt surreal, like something from a movie.

Your wife is attacked and your dog is the one that saves the day.

Neither Claire nor I will ever forget that day.

If Theo and I were tight before the job with Claire, we got even tighter after that. I was so proud and felt like I had a debt to settle with him: I promised I'd never let anything happen to him but it was a promise I'd struggle to keep.

We had a run of night shifts in the coming months and every job we were called on Theo aced and solved. Track or detain, he executed everything I asked of him brilliantly. I couldn't do any wrong with him, it seemed:

everything we went after he found and everyone we went up against he won.

A few days after Claire's attack we were called to a really nasty assault in Oldham town centre: a member of the public had been attacked. We were given a registration of a car – they believed the attackers had made off and Theo and I were on our way to the scene when a car matching the description but not the number plate drove past, going the opposite direction. The last three digits of the number plate were different, but I'd been doing the job long enough to be sure it was the car we were looking for.

In the aftermath of a vicious attack it's not uncommon for victims to get mixed up or forget details. When I asked comms whether they were sure about the number plate, they weren't. I put the lights on the van and turned around but rather than stop, which is what most people do when they have nothing to hide, it quickly turned into a high-speed pursuit before the assailants ditched the car and ran off into a housing estate.

It was a little after 3 a.m. and I gave the challenges but they didn't stop so I sent Theo in and followed on my two legs while he gained ground on his four. When I got round an alleyway, I saw one of the lads disappearing over a fifteen-foot fence. Theo took it in a single leap and

I felt like a proud dad at sports day. He cleared it fast but then the realisation set in that I'm 5ft 7in and had little chance of clearing it as quickly as he'd done. I was struggling to see how I'd follow and get into the garden on the other side of the wall.

As I heard Theo get hold of the lad, my predicament was that I couldn't get in. Shouting that I was coming, I clambered up the fence. I managed to get in and called Theo off.

The lad was shocked – he was on the floor in bits and had wet himself.

'How the hell did he get into this garden?'

But Theo was an elite. There was nothing that could beat him: no wall too tall, no track too tough. Theo was zeroed to me. He'd become exactly what I wanted and needed. He was incredible, a fantastic specimen of police dog, who absolutely doted on me – I couldn't have asked for more. Everything we went up against came right and went our way, it seemed.

A month or so after the Oldham town centre assault, the Tactical Vehicle Response Unit (TVRU) made it known they wanted a dog handler on their unit. Our dog vans aren't made to be fast so where time is of the essence and an assailant runs off after abandoning a car following a high-speed chase, we were turning up late with the odds stacked against us and the criminals with at least a ten-minute head start. The logical thinking was that if a dog handler was in a TVRU vehicle, they could be on scene fast and improve the outcome of the searches and chases.

Theo and I were selected for a three-month secondment to the TVRU. We'd be partnered with a driver who'd do all the hard work of driving the vehicle in the high-speed chases but we'd be able to move fast on the scene and make a difference to the outcomes. There was a team of twelve handlers on rotation with the unit but Theo and I got to go first. It was a huge honour and combined my two major loves, dogs and fast cars. I was in my element and loved it.

Claire was back at work one week after the attack and relieved to be back in uniform. I'd try and talk to her about the attack sometimes, but she understandably didn't feel like reliving it and would reassure me she was fine. We were still living with her mum and dad but, rather than a chore, it was ace. All four of us loved it and we were saving a fortune towards a house of our own and had actively started to look for one. We'd been there over twelve months and, while we loved it, neither of us wanted to outstay our welcome. We'd seen a few houses we liked but nothing we'd wanted to make an offer on.

As spring segued into summer, we developed a routine where we'd work hard but make sure we had as much fun as possible at the weekend. The kids were thriving, Eryn was due to start school in the September and they loved living with their grandparents. Julie, Claire's mum, would cook for us if we wanted it or we could cook for ourselves – it was like a lengthened holiday because there was so much help and support on hand.

Every Friday, we'd have a curry night and I'd be the one who cooked it each week. My beef madras was always the one everyone requested and, if I was on shift, I'd make sure I'd make it before I went to work, then eat mine when I came home.

Claire and I have always been passionate cyclists, and one warm long July weekend we decided we'd head out on the bikes. We loved cycling but rarely got to go together because of the kids. Eryn was playing in the garden with Claire's mum and we'd planned to cycle for an hour or so and then come back and have a barbecue. I was on Strava, a social media network for people who like their sports, and wanted to get a segment record and beat my friend who was the current holder.

It started out absolutely perfectly. The sun was shining, and we did a few gentle warm-up miles as we headed towards the start of the segment. I increased my speed

– Claire knew I was going for the segment and we'd agreed she'd catch up. I was in the zone and going at 42mph when the cleat on my shoe broke. My foot came off the pedal and within a split second I was hurtling over the top of the handlebars straight into a curb. My helmet smashed against the concrete, followed by my shoulder and I went face down in gravel on the edge of the road until I stopped moving.

Claire saw it happen but was moving too fast to stop. Luckily, no cars were coming or I'd have been instantly flattened. While she came to a stop and turned around to race back to me, a runner who'd seen it happen came over and tried to drag me out of the road. He said the noise had been horrific and he'd thought I'd been hit by a car. When he picked me up under my arms, I heard my shoulder and collarbone crack. Despite white-hot pain making me feel nauseous, the first thought in my head was about work and about Theo. It's daft I know, but it's true. The runner called an ambulance while Claire, who'd arrived breathless, begged me to stay still and not move. She was worried sick, but called a friend to come and get what was left of my bike.

For the next twenty minutes I drifted in and out of consciousness until I arrived at the hospital. I could see I was covered in gravel rash, a thousand tiny cuts covering every exposed area of skin. My clothes had been cut off me and while the pain was unimaginable, all I could think about was work and how long I might have to be off. Theo had been doing so well. To halt that and have him in kennels all day made me instantly worried we'd undo some of the good work. I'd just made it onto the TVRU and we were the most formidable partnership on the force.

I was X-rayed and had a break in my arm and collarbone. They wanted to put me in a sling while they decided whether to let it heal or pursue a surgical fix. Claire was in the cubicle with me and as the nurse readied herself to attempt to put the sling on, Claire went out into reception to call her mum, explain what had happened and make sure Eryn and Ben were okay.

I've got a pretty high pain threshold – it goes with the territory of being a dog handler, whether it's getting a nip from Theo by accident or getting something over the head from someone you're trying to catch. The simple act of trying to get a cloth sling on me was too much, though. I asked if I could lie down and do it because the pain was so intense.

The nurse sat me down on a plastic chair to see if we could do it that way. The last thing I remember is her asking me if I was okay if we tried again. Somehow I managed to get the word 'no' out before collapsing face first off the chair and onto the floor. My face took the brunt of the fall and I ended up with bruising, but because my arm had taken another bash, the bone I'd broken was now threatening to break the skin right on my collarbone. I'd managed to break it while riding, then split it down the middle falling off a chair in A&E.

At this point Claire came in. 'What the hell have you done now?' she asked, incredulous and getting a little impatient. It was a totally avoidable injury and she knew it. If I hadn't been so competitive with my friend, we'd be lighting the barbecue coals with a beer in hand by now. Instead we were stuck in a busy A&E unit on one of the warmest days of the year.

Another X-ray confirmed I'd made it worse by falling off the chair. I was told surgery involving screws and plates might be the best option but they wanted to give it a few days and have another surgeon consult before they made the final decision. It sounded instantly like the surgical route would get me back to work fastest but the doctors wanted me to come back to the fracture clinic for some follow-up assessments while they decided.

Claire took me home and gave me a pep talk on the way. She knew I was heartbroken – I didn't want to take

Theo to the kennels, I wanted to turn up for the night shift I was expected on the next day. She could see the frustration in me but told me we'd fix it and get me back as soon as we could.

The next day I begged the surgeon for the operation but he told me I'd be better off healing naturally. I was told to come back in two weeks but he might as well have taken my warrant card off me.

For two whole weeks I was in a foul mood. I couldn't walk Theo without Claire's help. I couldn't cook, clean or tidy either – I felt like I couldn't do anything at home and what I was doing was taking me three times as long because I only had one arm to use. Frustration was inevitable but I couldn't shake it off.

My shoulder and collarbone were in agony but the gravel rash that had scabbed over wasn't far behind. Every time I'd get goosebumps or get it wet, it would feel like it split and start stinging.

I wasn't sleeping and I stayed downstairs every night on the sofa, snatching a few minutes' sleep here and there so Claire could sleep uninterrupted instead of having me restless and in pain next to her. I'd sneak outside to see Theo and sit with him for hours at a time. I hated being useless and I felt that on every level – I couldn't take care of my family or my dog.

To add insult to injury, Claire and I had an offer accepted on a house we'd looked at a couple of days before we'd gone for our bike ride. The sellers wanted things to move fast so Claire had started packing our boxes from her mum and dad's house, and all I could do was watch and try and help with my one good hand.

Inevitably, with my frustration and boredom and the impending stress of a house move, things started heading south. I wasn't easy to be around and Claire was understandably anxious at the timing of everything. It was a needless accident and it had happened because I was competitively trying to get a segment record that I absolutely didn't need. I put myself in harm's way every day at work and Claire always accepted that, but with an impending house move and a new start, I'd put myself at risk because I was competitive, because I had an ego. Though kind and sympathetic to me, she was also having to do everything herself at such a crucial time for us both.

After two weeks I begged the surgeon again for an operation. He reluctantly agreed and I was admitted. My sister Suzanne (who as I've said is a doctor) had looked at the X-rays when I emailed them to her and concurred surgery would fix me faster.

One ray of sunshine while I was waiting to go down for my general anaesthetic was a guy whose face I recognised being admitted. He was screaming the odds about how much pain he was in, having been bitten by a police dog, and I recognised him as a petty repeat offender. While it made me smile briefly, it also reminded me of how much I missed working.

On 1 August 2015, I went under general anaesthetic. I had eight screws fitted in my shoulder and arm and a titanium plate. Home the same day, I felt a million times better instantly, but was told I'd be off for twelve weeks.

I called the sergeant and said I'd be back in eight weeks, if not sooner.

While Claire was kind, Theo was nothing but tender as I recovered. He was so gentle but I was bored – I hated not doing anything and I felt guilty I couldn't help with the house move. I felt like I'd ruined everything. The summer was passing by fast and I wasn't able to do any of the fun things we had planned.

Claire had to move house pretty much on her own as I couldn't lift anything much heavier than a teacup. Theo was languishing when he should have been catching baddies and because of those ingredients I was almost constantly in a bad mood.

On 19 August, we moved house with the help of family and friends. By the start of September, I was so thoroughly sick of watching Claire unpack and sort everything, I decided to see if ignoring it and carrying on as normal would work. Very slowly, I started building Theo's new kennel. It took twice as long to measure and cut the wood because I had only the one good hand but finally I was doing something myself and not sitting and watching while everyone else worked on around me.

Claire would roll her eyes at me using my knees to hold bits of wood together while I used the nail gun or holding a tape measure in my mouth but she knew I'd had enough and needed to do something that would make me feel useful. She had sorted us as a family in the house but it didn't feel like a home until Theo had his space sorted too.

As I gained more mobility and strength in my arm and shoulder, my mood lifted and it finally felt like we'd hit the patch we'd always strived for. We'd never owned a house together before: it was our dream, our happy ever after. We had the remnants of the summer to enjoy. I was winning at life and was sure we were at the start of the most incredible times of our lives.

I finally got back to work in the November and was barely back a week when I was asked if I wanted to take on a Spaniel. The German Shepherd is the traditional breed for the type of police work I was doing, but Spaniels have incredible noses – it's why they're often used as drug detection dogs. This one, though, would be trained as a cadaver dog: he'd be trained to smell and detect decomposing human remains and blood.

It wasn't made clear immediately that he'd be mine forever. I was asked to take him on and train him, but I knew once I let him through the door, he'd be in my heart. Sevvy was three months old and he was beautiful. For me he represented a new challenge – something completely different to what I'd done before – and I couldn't wait.

I didn't call Claire or check – after all, he might not be staying. Instead, I decided to rock up at home with him and see how things went from there.

I called Claire when I was outside the house and asked her to come out, but she instantly knew, 'There'd better not be another bloody dog in that van …'

'This is Sevvy …'

She melted and Sevvy moved in.

12

ERYN INSTANTLY ADORED SEVVY. He was a ball of fluff, playful as anything, and she decided he was hers and Theo was mine. She'd started school and loved every second but couldn't wait to get back every day and do some more training with Sevvy. We'd take him up to Hough End or the local field and work on recall and scent training. She was a fantastic handler and she and Sevvy formed an instant bond.

His training would include learning to search for drugs, cash, firearms, explosives and dead bodies, which is what he'd specialise in. He'd be trained in human decomposition and blood. I didn't tell Eryn the specifics, just that he'd find people. I was to train him, work Theo while I was doing it and expose him to as much of the world as I could.

The first night, Claire asked where he'd sleep. I put him in with Theo, half-wondering if I'd wake to find Theo picking bits of Sevvy out of his teeth, but I needn't have worried – their bond was instant and Theo absolutely adored him. He treated Sevvy like a best mate and a toy rolled into one. I could tell he thought Sevvy was a present for him, the best thing I'd ever brought home for him.

Theo had always been affectionate to me, but seeing him affectionate with another dog was amazing. Within minutes, the puppy in Theo was drawn out by this cheeky little Spaniel who wouldn't take no for an answer. Theo pretended to be a stern police dog who wouldn't be drawn into frolicking with a puppy but soon they were playing together beautifully.

Where anyone could apply to the Dog Unit to be a general-purpose handler, only internal candidates could apply for a search dog. Before you moved on to having a search dog that specialised in one of the areas of search, you had to cut your teeth with a German Shepherd-type dog.

While I was training Sevvy, my boss asked for expressions of interest from all the handlers: whoever was keen to have a second dog had to let him know. Without hesitation, I put my name down – I hadn't realised how much I'd enjoy having two police dogs, but made it clear I was only interested in the body side, the cadaver side. It really floated my boat. I knew it was a risk and I knew it meant I could lose Sevvy if they decided he should specialise in one of the other search areas, but it grabbed my attention so much it was a risk I thought worth taking. It was a long shot but I hoped they'd see Sevvy and I had a natural bond and decide to make him a cadaver dog so he could stay with me.

I've always loved helping people – it's the sole reason I'm a policeman because I like making streets safer, I like putting people in prison who have caused harm. The thought of being able to return dead loved ones to those who missed them instantly caught my imagination. Helping to bring that closure was something I desperately wanted to experience. It sounds evangelical but I believe I'm here for a reason. I enjoy the success of the jobs we do, but I'm here to help people. It's the reason I became a police dog handler and, for me, it's the most satisfying element of the entire job.

I trained Sevvy every second I had. I'd work Theo then train Sevvy. Initially, you get them addicted to a tennis ball. With Sevvy, that wasn't hard. He came on every single job I did with Theo, and when Theo had finished whatever the job was I'd put him in the van for some water. I'd get Sevvy out and let him have a look around, whether it was on a building site, the airport, the train station. I'd call him 'Little Man' and let him have a good sniff round everything – I wanted him to have experience and exposure to everything imaginable so when the time came to train him for blood and victim recovery he wouldn't find anything a distraction.

I spent weeks speaking to former dog handlers and getting advice from them too. I wanted to steal a march on his training: if he was to be a body dog, if he was to be *my* body dog, he'd be the best in the business. I'd make certain of it.

By the time Christmas 2015 came, we were exhausted from the year we'd had. From Claire's attack to my accident, it had been one hell of a time. We had the most amazing Christmas in our new house together. Claire worked Christmas Eve but Christmas Day was perfect.

New Year's Eve came around and we were having a party at our house. The New Year's Eve mantle had passed from Claire's parents onto us and we were both excited. We had everything sorted – a huge curry, a huge chilli, beer, wine, nibbles … We invited the neighbours. It was supposed to set the benchmark for a huge party every year.

I was training Sevvy at the kennels at the end of my shift and one of the other lads I worked with – Rob – asked me to help him train his dog in some bite work. It wasn't unusual to help each other out, we quite often did, so I agreed and put Sevvy in kennels before putting the sleeve on.

We were going to do a concealed bite, which is where you hide a thinner sleeve under your normal clothing, the thought process being that it's easy to train a dog to bite a sleeve they know won't hurt the owner they love but asking them to bite when they think you're not wearing a sleeve is where the hard work comes in. As a handler, you need them not to think but to follow your instruction.

I started running, Rob's dog Zac caught up with me and locked on with a good bite. I started to slow down but as I did he adjusted on me, missed the sleeve and I felt his teeth hit the bone in my wrist. You can't scream in pain when that happens and you can't panic because that would undo a lot of the training you've worked on. As handlers, it's funny when you're bitten. Of course, it hurts, but you know you have to stay positive otherwise the dog will think it's done something wrong when it hasn't and it might be deterred from ever biting again, which is of course not what you want when you've already put in weeks and weeks of training.

I felt light-headed with the pain but in a squeaky voice I managed to praise him and tell him he was a good boy before his owner called him back.

Exercise over, Zac thought he'd done a great job.

The minute he was away from me I fell to the floor. I didn't want to look at my wound, I knew it was bad, so I put the palm of my hand over the top. Rob came over and asked if I was okay. I explained what had happened and took my hand away for us both to see how bad it was. There was a huge hole in my wrist and we both said the words 'A&E' at exactly the same time before laughing.

So I went in and had it cleaned. I knew they couldn't stitch it – you don't stitch dog bites unless you absolutely have to, because as I've said before there's so much bacteria in their mouths. You're better off cleaning the wound out initially and then stitching if you have to.

Around 3 o'clock in the afternoon, I got to the hospital. I was seen pretty quickly and when the consultant came in, he put his fingers right up inside my wrist. An excruciating pain shot the length of my arm.

'Can you feel that?' he asked.

'Yes, I can bloody feel it!' I replied, my eyes watering.

'Everything is intact then, we'll give you a tetanus shot and butterfly stitch it.'

I went home and Claire was about as sympathetic as the A&E doctor had been. She basically told me it was my fault and had a good laugh at my expense. Having grown up with a dog handler as a dad, she knew the occupational hazards involved in training dogs and the injury wasn't as serious as it could have been. We still had the party but I couldn't do a lot. Despite the injury, it was a perfect night and Claire and I rang in the New Year with a kiss and excitement about what the next year of our lives had in store for us.

Theo and I hit the ground running in 2016. I didn't know it at the start but it would be one of his best years ever. He began the year as successfully as he'd ended the previous one: he was catching bad people, his bite work was perfect, he was becoming a dog with a reputation – everyone knew who he was across the force.

In April, we were called to an armed robbery. Theo started a track and then lost it. We went back to the beginning and started again. It was unusual for him to lose a track and I could feel my stress levels starting to rise. Undeterred, we went back to the car that had been abandoned so he could pick up the scent and we started again.

A few minutes later, he lost the scent again. It was unlike him and my stress gave way to anger: he knew how to do this, he'd done it hundreds of times and was always successful. I couldn't figure out why he was losing it, but I was hugely frustrated with him. I took him back to the van to give him some water and ended up throwing some over him – I was angry with him for losing it, especially because I knew how good he could be.

While he drank, I sat down and had a word with myself. I was stressed because he'd lost the track and that feeling had gone right down the lead to him. He hadn't let me down, I'd let myself down and I'd let him down. I apologised to him and gave him a fuss: 'I'm sorry, son, I'm really sorry. I shouldn't have shouted at you and that was unkind and unfair. I know you're doing your best and I know it's my fault you've lost it, so if you can forgive me, why don't we go back and start again, no pressure, okay?'

He licked my face to signal all was forgiven and back on the scene I decided to try a different tack. I was used to saying a few words to Theo every time he tracked but it felt like this time he needed more than that. I'd unsettled him a bit and while I'd apologised, it meant nothing to him, but I could show him I was sorry by really praising him while he tracked.

We got back to the car and started again. This time I praised him effusively, telling him he was fantastic and giving him a stroke while he pushed on. It resulted in success, an arrest and from then on I have a constant stream of conversation with Theo when he tracks.

A few days later, we were called to a break-in. I was working the same shift as Claire, which happened occasionally when we couldn't move things. Her mum and dad were at home with Eryn and Ben.

By the time I got there, the firearms team were there. There are egos that go with certain parts of the police. Ask anyone if dog handlers have big egos and they'll say yes, and while I think they're wrong, I doubt you'll find any police officer who won't agree with me when I say the firearms teams have egos too.

'We don't need you, we need a firearms dog,' was the greeting I received before I'd even got Theo out the car.

'Okay, fine, no problem,' I replied.

I knew better than to try and sell Theo to them; I was on the scene and if they wanted to wait for a firearms dog, I'd get out of the way and leave them to it. I was back in the van just as another armed robbery came in at a swanky bar in town so I turned on my lights and got there as fast as I could. There was an abandoned car fitting the number plate we'd been given by eyewitnesses but whoever had been inside it was long gone.

Very long gone.

I decided to see what Theo could track – I didn't expect to find anyone or anything as there'd been loads of foot traffic through the area and around the car that was now cordoned off, but it was worth a shot. His new style of tracking had become successful so it was worth a punt before we ended the shift. I put him on a long line and chatted to him. He set off like a different dog, tracking brilliantly. He found the knife, the balaclava and all the clothing that had been used in the armed robbery. He didn't find the assailants but to me it was a better result – he'd shown me he could find things other than people.

Each item was in a different location and he'd persevered. He found tights first with eye holes cut out (yes, criminals still use them), then a knife further down the track and, finally, a balaclava. He'd found the three items spread over half a mile and, while he could have laid down, signalling the end of the search when he got the tights, he'd pushed on to exhaust every possibility and been successful twice more. I was so impressed he hadn't stopped at the first find. He'd signalled he'd found something by lying down, but the minute the tights were bagged, he got up and carried on. I hadn't trained or taught him to do that, he did it of his own accord. It was like he understood there might be more to come.

Theo was developing a drive himself, he was becoming unstoppable.

The same month we were called to another armed robbery with the TVRU, this time at a bar called the Laundrette in Chorlton. They had burst in, armed with swords and machetes, and forced the staff at knifepoint to go downstairs and empty the safe. A car had escaped but we had intelligence suggesting it had been dumped in another part of the city. I went there with the report that six males had abandoned the vehicle and run off. Sure enough, the car was where we'd been told it would be with no one in it and the doors all closed.

Whoever had abandoned it had done so in a hurry.

Normally, I wouldn't have thought too much about what we'd find or whether we'd be successful, but Theo was on such a high and his tracking had come on so much, I was incredibly optimistic. It was an urban search. I got him out and put him on the long line, then I took him to the driver's side of the car for him to get the scent and gave him the command 'Seek on!'

Concrete surfaces are the hardest to track on – we call them a 'hard surface track', and the scent on hard surfaces can dissipate really quickly. If it's frosty or icy, the scent will stick to it, but when it's bone-dry the scent doesn't hang around. Hard surface tracks are more difficult because the dog has to work harder to get the scent and retain it as it's dissipating. Grass and mud retain the scent and can be easier to work, but in typical Theo style his nose hit the ground and it was like a switch had gone off. He was off in seconds while I struggled to keep up. I knew he had the scent and, while I encouraged him on, I was excited about what he might find.

The more the track went on, the more I knew he was onto something. I tried to stay calm and encouraging, but it was dawning on me that there were eyewitness reports of six men and I was first on the scene – the only one tracking so far. Of course, I wanted him to be successful but what we'd find was concerning: there was every chance we'd be hugely outnumbered if we did find the men. There was also a huge likelihood they'd fled in different directions but it was something I was wary of as Theo kept pushing on.

He took me to a main junction at the edge of the housing estate. There was a dog van to the left, a huge relief for me because I knew I wasn't the only one tracking anymore, but Theo's reaction surprised me. Normally when a dog sees a dog van they get attracted and distracted by it, but this time Theo was nose down and straight over the junction, he'd barely glanced up. He took me into a road with a small row of bungalows on either side. As we headed along the road, my adrenaline was flowing.

There was a silver car outside one of the bungalows with a young lad in it on his phone. He was a million miles away and didn't see me on the other side of the road, but something didn't look right.

The bungalow he was outside had a window open and it was a cold night. The blinds were flapping in the breeze and it struck me as being unusual.

Theo made a move to try and get into the window but I pulled him back before he could. His nose had led us here and he'd indicated the track would finish if he was allowed through the window.

I hid behind a wall and looked inside: there were three adult men getting changed and throwing money around like they were in some Hollywood movie. Shocked and delighted, I couldn't contain my excitement: 'Bloody hell, Theo, you've found them, you've bloody found them!' I whispered and gave him a stroke, my heart pounding.

Theo had found the team of armed robbers.

What I was feeling inevitably went down the lead. Theo was whimpering, he was expecting the challenges to be issued, but I couldn't with so many of them. There was a chance he'd fare okay against three but it was unlikely even with the element of surprise on our side.

I whispered on the radio that I thought I'd found them. The firearms team were close by and patrol cars were out too so by the time reinforcements arrived, it was like an army invasion on this quiet little street.

The lad in the car almost wet himself when everyone descended and I guessed – correctly, as it turned out – that he was the getaway driver.

After giving Theo a huge fuss, I started walking back to the car. I bumped into a friend at the top of the road, another dog handler. Theo was pulling on his lead towards a fence and, while I knew we'd only found three of the six armed robbers, I presumed the others were long gone in another direction.

I couldn't have been more wrong.

As I turned towards the fence, a lad appeared at the top of it, obviously about to pull himself over until he saw two police officers and a police dog on the other side of it. He swore loudly and dropped back down so I sent Theo in, following immediately behind him myself.

I thought there was only the one lad who'd been trying to get away but another was behind him, who would have come over the wall after his pal. Theo knocked one flying with the full force of his body and detained the other one at the end of the bungalow. It was utter chaos – there were fences being broken by the firearms unit, who were on the scene, there were people coming out of their houses, but Theo ignored all that. He was locked onto the lad in question and he detained him. The fellow handler I'd seen while Theo was tracking detained the last guy at around the same time we got our two.

All six were detained and arrested, and if it wasn't for Theo none of them would ever have been found. He made the world safer by finding five dangerous armed robbers who had all been doing it for years. In the subsequent trial, Theo was praised by the counsel Anthony Cross QC, who called for him to be honoured by Greater Manchester Police. He spoke for fifteen minutes about Theo. A detective friend called me afterwards to tell me what he'd said and I was completely overwhelmed. It's never been about accolades or awards or recognition, but knowing Theo was held in such high esteem by someone so professional felt amazing. I told Theo about it excitedly, regaling him as best I could with what the QC had said and, while it made no odds to him, I was delighted for him. It remains another one of Theo's best ever jobs and if I could go back and relive it again, I would.

Afterwards, I went back to the nick and wanted to scream from the rooftops what he'd done. Instead, I finished the shift, wrote the report and texted Claire, who was delighted and amazed in equal measure. She was always proud of us, but being the heroes of the hour was an incredible feeling.

13

I LOVED THE THRILL I GOT from working Theo. The job I'd always wanted to do felt like it was the best it could possibly be. I thrived on how well we were doing and of course Claire was someone who knew what I was talking about when I regaled her with our stories because she'd grown up with her dad on the Dog Unit.

In May 2016, a few months after Theo's wonder job, we were called to a track in Glossop, Derbyshire. I'd been working the night shift and it had been pretty quiet. The local constabulary shouted up on the radio that there had been a cash machine robbery and the car had made off. I knew the exact area it had happened in – there was basically one road they could be on, one road to take you in and out of the area. I also knew when we put the lights on and set off we stood a good chance of finding them if we mobilised quickly enough. It's not unusual for neighbouring forces to help each other out, so I shouted up that I'd give it a go and soon I was on my way with Theo.

It was a rural area and the couple of cars that had come with me left after twenty minutes, bored and unable to find them. That's one of the many great things about being a dog handler, though: when other police officers have to rely on intelligence or eyewitness reports, or calls from the public, we don't have to. All we need is one lucky break and we can deploy the sixth sense: the dog we're handling. If a police officer finds an abandoned car, they can swab it and run the swabs and forensics can get involved, but when a police dog is shown an abandoned car you know you're likely to start a track, end up in a chase and, hopefully, an arrest.

As the other cars headed back to their divisions, Theo and I continued to drive around the area while we chatted. We were driving round some back lanes when, out the corner of my eye, I spotted the rear lights of a parked car matching the description of the vehicle. I parked up and saw the vehicle was empty so I radioed some assistance and prepared Theo for the track to try and find whoever it was who had abandoned the vehicle. I was looking at the car when a figure wearing a balaclava appeared on the other side of it. Neither of us expected to see each other and I let out a little squeal. I ran for the van to get Theo while the lad in the balaclava took off.

Sprinting back to the van, I issued challenges and when the lad kept running I let Theo give chase. He had at least thirty seconds on Theo and I saw him disappear down an alleyway and take a sharp right out onto open land. Theo hooked a right into a garden and I was convinced they were hiding there. The reality was that they'd built up lots of scent by hiding there for a few minutes but had made off before we got there and, by the time I figured it out, they had a few minutes on us.

I got Theo out of the garden and let him go. He put his head to the ground and went, with me a few seconds behind him. It was pitch-black and I couldn't see the hand in front of my face. Less than ten seconds later, I heard screaming: Theo had done it again, or so I thought. When I finally caught up and shone my torch, though, I realised Theo hadn't detained anyone: he'd found his way into a pig pen and couldn't get out.

Exasperated, but also seeing the funny side, I freed him and sent him back on again to continue the track. This time he took me in a different direction and I could see his body language getting more animated after just a few seconds. He continued tracking and dragged himself through a bracken bush, signalling the lad had gone the same way.

I've always talked to Theo on every track, but sometimes I've been known to swear at him a bit. When dragged through a bush, you get cut to ribbons and you can spend hours taking thorns out of your hands, but the dogs we handle get so excited by what they're scenting they don't wait and think, 'Hang on, is this the best way for me to go or is there an easier route?', they just go ahead and you have to follow. It's all well and good tracking on roads or through town centres but Theo had a habit of dragging me through bushes and bracken where I'd be cut to shreds or through streambeds where I'd be caked in mud and water. On those jobs it's always easy to have a bit of a go at him – in the nicest possible way.

That night was one of those times: 'You'd better be bloody right, you big idiot! If I'm following you, getting cut to shreds and you're after a pig pen again, I'll be bloody cross with you ...' He was still going and, after disappearing through another thorny bush, he caught the lad we'd seen by the car.

Despite a melee in a pig pen, he'd persevered and tracked him.

No one knew where we were but we'd done it. It took us a while to get back to the van, but once there I gave

Theo some fuss. I was buzzing. He'd done it again. He'd given me what I loved: success.

I unclipped him to go for a wee and he trotted off. Mid-wee, though, he walked off, which was unlike him. We were beside the van and he wandered a few yards down the road and lay down on the corner of two streets, an indication he'd found something. I walked over to see what he'd found and he was lying down right next to the key to the stolen car.

As far as his training was concerned, his job was done, he'd found the baddie. He'd finished what he was supposed to do and been successful. But Theo was more than just a trained police dog, he had learned to think for himself and was now an amazing police dog. He knew when he got that scent it pertained to the job we'd just been on – he'd remembered the scent and linked it to the one coming from the car key. Despite the fact his lead was off and we were back at the van he caught a whiff of something, which told him the job wasn't over. I couldn't have trained him in that and I defy any handler who says they could.

Theo was fast becoming the ultimate police dog and if you'd done something wrong and he was tracking you, you simply couldn't get away from him. It was one of the only jobs in all his service where we managed to get ourselves a complaint, though. Seemingly, the farmer didn't appreciate a big German Shepherd exciting his pigs in the dead of the night. Can't think why!

Theo had done such a good job that track, I treated us to a cheese sandwich and ready-salted crisps, his favourite and a treat he got when he did especially well. I bought them from a petrol station and we sat in the van while we waited for another job to come in. It wasn't anything unusual for me to have a bite and then him to have a bite of the same sandwich. I know that's not to everyone's taste but we shared everything. There was a couple sat in their car next to me who couldn't hide their disgust at me and a dog sharing the same sandwich. I realised then maybe we should have separate halves rather than sharing both halves.

While Theo's special treat was a cheese sandwich, his real treat was coming to work. The second we got out, he'd sprint to the van to get started. Whatever I felt went down the lead and the more I became addicted to working him and our success, the more he did too. I was starting to spend longer than I probably should have at work. It's not unusual for handlers to come back to kennels around half an hour before the end of the shift to get the van washed down, their dog fed and watered and everything put back where it should be, but Theo and I were starting to spend every minute of our shift in the car or on jobs and then we'd come back and clean down afterwards. It meant we were adding a good hour onto our working days or nights, something Claire – understandably – found difficult.

Claire wasn't jealous of Theo, though she worried my work–life balance wasn't a healthy one, but when she tried to talk to me about it, I refused to listen. It's not like we were doing anything bad – after all, the more time we spent on shift, the more baddies we were taking off the streets – but with so much time at work, there was little headspace for much else.

Moving out of her parents' house and buying our own place together also meant we started working opposite shifts again because her mum and dad weren't on hand to babysit and do school runs so we could work the same shifts. The carefree existence we'd had courtesy of them was starting to feel like it was a long time ago.

The amount of quality time we spent together as either a couple or a family dwindled too. Claire and I had enjoyed date nights, bike rides, long walks and day trips when we lived with her mum and dad. Now we barely saw one another and, when we did, days were spent decorating or getting the house exactly how we wanted it. Rather than tackle the situation head-on or make some changes, though, we both ignored it and I threw myself into work while she balanced work and the kids.

Theo and I were working a nightshift at the end of May that started out like any other. We had a call to track a male who had stabbed his female partner in the pub, then run off. He'd tried to kill her, aiming for her throat, but she'd moved and he'd stabbed her collarbone so it wouldn't go through. Fellow drinkers at the pub had disarmed him, but he had run off, clearly inebriated and on something.

We were on our way to the pub to start the track when we received another call from comms. The man had turned up at the family home. His partner was on her way to hospital in an ambulance but their three children were at home in bed and he was pouring petrol from a canister through the letter box of the closed and locked front door.

Straight away, I knew this was a different type of job. Division didn't shout for a police dog once he'd been located, but I shouted up and said I'd go. I knew they thought a police dog would be useless but I had a plan and I knew Theo would be instrumental in it: I asked them not to let anyone else go near him until we got there.

There were so many scenarios I'd run through in my head over the years I'd had Theo. I'd thought about all sorts of ways I could lose him, from injury to torsion – a potentially fatal medical condition where their stomach twists – to being run over tracking through an urban area, but I felt a shiver down my spine as we approached the address. I knew this was a serious job and I knew with petrol a lot could be at risk. I love Theo and I'd lay down my life for him, but I'd also lay his life down for others.

If you go to work as a police officer and you're killed in the line of duty, everyone is affected – your force family, your actual family, your loved ones, friends, neighbours. It's a huge hole left in everyone's life. If my police dog Theo was killed in the line of duty, the hole left would be in my life but not everyone else's.

Every day, I carry that burden: I worry about it every time I lace up my boots before a shift. I'd sacrifice myself for Theo if it came down to it, but I also knew it was my job to realise that he might have to be the sacrifice in order to save others. I was looking at a scenario where I'd use Theo and he could possibly be about to lay down his life for the force he'd served so faithfully. I knew how much he'd developed and I gave him a pep talk on the way: 'You ready for this, son? It's a big job and we don't know what's going to happen but you know I love you, don't you? We've got to do this and I need you to be switched on, okay? Keep your wits about you and make sure you're focused. There's no choice here, we've got to do what we've got to do.'

We rocked up at the scene and there were two officers keeping their distance. The suspect was near his front door, petrol canister in hand. The entire area smelled like a petrol forecourt, thick with the scent of gasoline. It was exactly the scenario I expected, but one I'd prayed we'd never come across.

Theo tried to jump on my lap and inadvertently set the sirens going. He was desperate to get into the job but where I'd hoped for a bit of stealth, clumsy Theo had other ideas. With the assailant just metres from the front door, there was a police officer around 10 metres away from him on either side. As I'd asked, both had kept their distance. One had a Taser gun in his hand but I asked him to step back – I knew if he tased him, we'd all go up like it was Bonfire Night.

The bloke was agitated, waving around the petrol canister while gesticulating wildly. He was on something, but it didn't take a genius to figure there wasn't a way he could come out of this unscathed. He was shouting and swearing and I had Theo under the collar, primed and ready.

The next few seconds went by in slow motion. I could feel Theo bristling, but it was unlike any scene we'd encountered before. I started issuing the challenges, not because I wanted to send Theo in, but because I desperately wanted the bloke to surrender. Despite me silently hoping and praying he'd come quietly and easily, though, he had no intention of surrendering. He was committed at that point: he'd already stabbed a woman and shown intent to harm his children, so he'd be looking at a custodial sentence even if he surrendered and he knew it. He wasn't coming easy and he wouldn't give in, no matter how much I wanted him to.

'Get hold of him and I'll sort it,' I whispered to Theo before I let him go. I was a few metres from him so I knew things would happen fast. It would take Theo a second to reach him but, as I let go of him, the bloke's right hand appeared out of his pocket with a lighter.

It was a Zippo and I saw the spark.

He flipped it and I've never seen a light and a flash like it. He was covered in petrol fumes and both he and Theo went up in a whoosh. I saw the stub of Theo's tail disappear into the ball of flames. The sound and the searing heat seemed to suck all the air in with it.

I was knocked back by the force of the flames but scrambled to my feet a second later. My first thought was, *Where's Theo?* He'd been set alight and, rather than detain the bloke, he had run off past one of the police officers.

The assailant was on fire. It looked like something you see in the movies but there was no sound coming from him. He went into his pocket and pulled a knife out. I rushed forward with another police officer just as Theo reappeared. Theo barged the other police officer out of the way and made straight for the suspect. In a split second, I realised he had somehow managed to put himself out and was back to finish what he started. Elation ran through me – my dog who'd been on fire was still alive – but that was closely followed by terror. I knew Theo was heading for a man who was on fire with a knife in his hand.

With a certainty I'd never seen before Theo latched on and made one of the best bites of his life. He got his right arm that had the knife in, disabling the bloke from using it on Theo or anyone else. He was still on fire, though, and I rushed in with another police officer to get him to the ground and try and put him out, as much for his own safety as Theo's.

Theo pushed the other police officer away with a growl. I'll never know what went through his head in that split second but I'm pretty sure he was keeping that lad out of harm's way. Theo knew he had the situation under control and he knew I was in it too. My dog was prepared to risk his own life and mine, but not another police officer's. We got the situation under control in a matter of seconds and, as I called Theo off, intervening officers took over.

I raced Theo back to the van as fast as I could. All I could smell was burning fur. Panting hard and whimpering, he had no whiskers or eyebrows left and was burned from the flash of the fumes with a very crispy nose. He hadn't been doused in petrol, but the fumes and the fact his fur was flammable had left him really sore.

Everyone was worried about us.

As the lad was carted off in an ambulance with the police in tow, shouts came over the radio and attending officers kept checking we were okay.

I got Theo straight to the vets and explained what happened. He was burned but not severely: he'd put himself out in a matter of seconds so had averted something worse happening with his own quick thinking.

To get him to calm down, I took him out for a walk. I got Sevvy out too and he kept licking him as if he could make it better. It was the dead of the night and I knew Theo needed the cool air on his skin and to relax a bit and calm down before I took him home. We both needed to process what had happened too and, as always, it was easier for us to do that when we were walking.

Theo disappeared out of my eyeline around a corner and I followed him, taking deep breaths and trying to come to terms with the job we'd just been on without crying. It's taken me a while to get over it, but I kept reminding myself we were both safe and Theo had no lasting damage.

When I rounded the corner, though, Theo was sat in the middle of three lads in their mid-twenties in track-suits. He growled at them and I called him over to me. As he sat at heel, I asked what they were doing.

'We're playing football, boss.'

'It's 2 a.m., you're not playing football here, are you?'

I was all over the place – I'd come here to decompress and calm down and Theo had found something. As I flicked back into handler mode, I was silently cursing him. Why did he have to find another potential job for us? Why couldn't he have just stuck with me and let the cold air soothe his burned skin? Why did he always have to look for jobs, for trouble? In that second I sympathised with Claire – I guessed she often thought the same thing about me. We hadn't been called to anything and while I was seriously suspicious about what they were doing, we had no cause or call to detain or question them.

I let them go into the night but the next day a call came in to say that some garages exactly where we'd been had been broken into. Theo was so switched on – even when he was supposed to be off after the worst shift of his life, he was a baddie magnet. He couldn't not keep his patch safe.

While we were both exhausted when we finished and finally got home around 7 a.m., Claire woke me early the next morning: the call-out and Theo being set on fire had made the papers.

'You could both have been killed …'

Before I could utter anything in my defence or Theo's, Claire gave me a dressing-down. I knew she was worried, she'd been terrified when she'd heard what happened. She loved me and I was Eryn and Ben's too; she adored Theo and the thought of losing us both that way had really scared her. I was sore and stiff and knackered, but I told her what had happened from our side. She ended up proud of us both, but tried to get me to promise I wouldn't risk Theo again – not a promise I could make.

The next day, I was on nights and arrived at work to an email from the division superintendent. She thanked me for our work the previous night and asked me to let her know Theo was okay.

For me it was a huge deal to get that care from so far up the chain and it dawned on me that I couldn't ever thank Theo enough. Yes, I could treat him and give him lots of love, but he'd never understand the gravitas of what he'd done. He didn't know the cause and effect. He didn't know there were kids safe in their beds thanks to him, that kids had their Christmas presents back because of him, that bad people were off the streets and in prison.

All. Because. Of. Him.

14

AS THEO AND I GREW EVER CLOSER, I saw less and less of Claire. Our shifts were still opposite to one another so we could keep up with family, house and child commitments, and the rare times we had weekends or time off together we were both tired and not really present with one another.

I'd put so much of myself into work. If I wasn't working Theo, I was training Sevvy. I'd spend hours reading about training and speaking to other handlers on different forces, asking for help and advice on making him the best cadaver dog Greater Manchester Police had ever seen. I was working long hours anyway and added overtime on top of that meant my already-long days were even longer.

When I wasn't working, Theo and Sevvy still needed two walks a day of around forty-five minutes a time.

There was cleaning out their kennel daily at home, their three meals a day to prep, not to mention the house-work, cleaning, tidying and washing school uniforms and mine and Claire's work clothes.

We went from being the couple who had enjoyed long walks and weekends away when we lived at her parents' to being two people cohabiting together, both in our own worlds with our own orbits. Occasionally, I'd try to talk about the growing distance between us but, looking back, I never chose the right times. When Claire had been on shift all day, I'd have been at home mulling things over and thinking about the best way forward and how we could recapture what we were fast losing. When she came in the door exhausted and just wanting to eat and sleep, I took it personally that she wouldn't open up to me.

I couldn't help but appraise our relationship and compare it to the other relationships in my life. I adored Eryn and Ben: they were fantastic kids and whatever I gave them in love and time came back to me in exactly the same way. Theo was my rock, my best friend – he gave me just as much as I gave him, the same with Sevvy.

Claire volunteered to work the majority of Christmas 2016 and, rather than say anything about it, her decision suited us both. I got the house ready for Christmas and enjoyed it all with Eryn, who still believed in Father Christmas.

Christmas is a busy time for the whole force but especially firearms so Claire was working long hours while I took time off. I'd spend evenings with Eryn upstairs, watching a movie or playing computer games with Ben, while Claire watched TV downstairs. We had her parents over for Christmas and while we had an amazing day – we were always able to stick a pin in our problems in company – we both knew things between us were at the lowest ebb they'd ever been since we'd married.

Claire worked New Year's Eve while I saw in the New Year with Ben and Eryn at her parents' house, and when she started her time off in January Theo and I were back on shift. We spent the spring like we'd spent the last few months of 2015: we were reliably on form, we knew each other inside out and our success rate was high.

In May 2016, shortly after Theo had been burned, with his new whiskers growing back, we were sent to South Yorks force for six weeks starting at the end of that month to finish the cadaver handling course. By then, it was a foregone conclusion that Sevvy would stay with me and I'd be a cadaver handler as well as a general-purpose handler. Theo had tested me and we were a team so now I'd work two dogs and see if I could get that bond and success rate with Sevvy I was fortunate enough to enjoy with Theo.

Working Sevvy would mean I wasn't anywhere near the coalface of crime, where both me and my dog had been hurt in the line of duty. Body dogs are called in when missing person inquiries or cases like that come to a dead end. Very rarely are there blue lights and drama because you're looking for someone who might have been dead for weeks or months. I figured Claire would be happier with me working Sevvy more and Theo less because I'd spend less time in harm's way. I couldn't control my marriage or the outcome of what might happen – or at least that's how it felt at the time – so I focused instead on what I could control and I could make Sevvy a fantastic little body dog.

The course itself was incredible. Theo came with me and stayed in South Yorks kennels while I trained Sevvy. The days started at 7 a.m. and you'd train your dog to recognise the scent of decomposition and blood. We use pig organs and bodies as they're chemically and biologically very similar to humans, so when they move into real service they know what they're searching for. The size of the blood cells is similar, the cell lifespan is the same, so decomposition happens at much the same rate in pigs as it does humans.

Sevvy was incredible – it was like Theo had given him a pep talk on what to do. A fantastic Spaniel and a brilliant body dog, he passed the course with flying colours. He was focused and his nose was incredible; everyone on the course knew he was something else. Yes, I'd worked with him and, yes, I'd trained him, but Sevvy was a natural talent: he'd done the work himself and I knew he'd change a lot of people's lives.

In June 2016, I did something I'd never have done at the start of my marriage to Claire.

I bought my dream car, a Subaru Impreza, and I didn't even tell her I was doing it.

It wasn't the right thing to do: Claire had work she wanted to get done on the house and we hadn't got a holiday planned, but stubbornness and selfishness can go hand in hand, and while I'd always dreamed of owning one, I half bought it to see what her reaction would be.

She didn't say a word about it.

* * *

We got back after the cadaver handling course in mid-July. Everything was pretty much as I'd left it. Claire and I both knew our relationship wasn't what it should be but it seemed neither of us had the courage or will to sit down and sort things out.

We spent a lot of time apart. Up until I'd got back from the course it had been because our shift patterns fell in a way that it was hard for us to spend time together but after the course, even if we had the choice to be together, we'd find something to do with friends or with the kids that meant we couldn't be together.

I'd take Theo and Sevvy with me to work every shift and, depending on the shout, I'd work with one of them. It was November 2016 when I had a shout for a job that would change everything.

I was on shift when we had a visit from a new inspector from the Professional Standards Practice (PSP) – the police's police, if you like. They investigate if there's ever a complaint from the public or an assailant about the way things are handled. There'd been rumblings for some time that we'd have to change the way we wrote statements as dog handlers. We'd write them in such a way that described what went on and what happened, and when we'd called our dogs back to our sides, but the injuries sustained were never described and the PSP wanted that to change so there was even more transparency. It seemed like a brilliant idea – we'd be covered even more than our usual statements and a lot of us handlers wondered why it had taken so long to change.

I met with the inspector, but within a few minutes I could feel myself start to bristle: he'd never handled a dog, never been out with us, and was telling us our jobs and practically how to do them. I asked what he wanted us to deliver.

'I want a job from start to finish caught on camera with evidence and rationale on why you've done everything. If you give me that, I'll teach you how to accept a complaint and you'll be bulletproof. If you're open and honest, it won't go to complaint level.'

A few weeks later, I was on shift when a shout came in for a track on Saddleworth Moor at Uppermill. If you're not familiar with the area, it's a tiny village, a beautiful area, but people mainly go there to commit crime because it's fairly wealthy and in the middle of nowhere.

It was two burglars who'd made off with jewellery and valuables. By the time Theo and I got on the scene, there'd already been a lot of footfall. Rural tracks can be difficult because there's so much natural scent, but Theo was his usual brilliant self. He started a track, then lost it. I took him back to the beginning and we started again. He kept finding it, only to lose it again. It was unlike him, but we persevered.

After an hour and a half, I was so frustrated. I hated not finding tracks. It didn't happen often with Theo because his success rate was so fantastic, but on the rare occasions it did, I'd get mad at myself and wonder whether I was doing something wrong or if I'd passed some stress down the lead to him. Our shift was ending so I left Uppermill and passed the job on to the day shift.

I was driving back to Hough End but as I got to Ashton-under-Lyne another report came in over the radio to say the burglars had been sighted on the open moor. I was sat at the lights in a foul mood – I hate people getting away from me, I get sombre and upset. You know they'll likely commit again and I always feel it's my fault.

I know Theo can find a track, *any* track. I know he's the best, so if he can't find one it's because I've put him in the wrong area or I've done something wrong. He's the strong part of the partnership, I'm the weak one when it comes to scent.

Things hadn't gone as they should have: the PSP meeting was still grating on me, I felt the Dog Unit was being persecuted and, despite our best efforts, we still weren't valued as we should have been. I remember the internal monologue I had with myself: 'Go home, Gareth, just go home. You're off-shift, this isn't your job, you've done your bit.'

I looked in the rear-view mirror and saw him looking at me: 'I bloody hate you, Theo, you know we don't have to do this?' I was in full-on rant mode. 'If you're going to look at me like that and make me go, you'd better be successful, do you hear me, T?' I put the blue lights on and, within minutes, we were at the place they'd been sighted and Theo was harnessed up, ready to go.

I met the bobby on the scene and he said he'd seen them on the moors. It seemed as good a chance as any and, with the camera on me, I started recording. I was chatting to Theo like I normally do, encouraging him on and telling him what a great job he was doing. We set off and the first bit of the track was up a steep hill. By the time we crested the ridge, I was blowing and knackered. Theo was tracking really well and I was doing everything I normally would. I had the inspector's words going through my head about getting everything on film when Theo lit off on a track using the entire length of his long lead: he had something and he was off!

I went with him, struggling to keep up. As I was running across moorland, I kept thinking, 'I'm in the middle of nowhere, no one would believe this dog is right. There's dense fog coming down, nothing has given any sign he's on the right track ...' Despite my negative thoughts, we pushed on. I knew to trust him and I knew he never let me down. I put my whole faith in him and followed his stubby little tail round every tree and bend.

About half an hour into the track, I came across a farmer, who asked what I was doing. I explained and we made small talk for a few seconds. Theo lay down next to me for a rest but, within seconds, he fired off and squeezed under a barbed-wire fence to our right. I shouted over my shoulder that I had to follow my dog and crawled, like Theo had, through the mud and under the fence. We went along the side of a dry stone wall and I radioed back to base to make sure someone was tracking my location and knew where I was because I had absolutely no idea.

After another half a mile, all of a sudden Theo lay down next to a pile of rocks: it was his sign he'd found something. I was obviously frustratingly slow on my two legs compared to his four because by the time I got to him, he was starting to paw at the ground. When I moved some of the rocks, at the bottom of a makeshift cairn was a man bag (a little satchel-type bag). I knew from the job when it was first called in that the assailants had a man bag.

It had a load of jewellery in it.

'How can you do this, Theo? Where and how did you find this? You're amazing, you're so smart …'

I was satisfied with what he'd done – it was a huge success to have gone over a mile on a rural track and found something that was buried, but before I could congratulate him any more, he was off again.

I thought the job was done, Theo had other ideas.

The faith I have in him is unquestionable so I followed suit. We tracked for another quarter of a mile at least. He took me to a farm, a beautiful posh farm. There was a set of steps covered in moss and Theo slipped going down them. I did the same and, as we picked ourselves up at the bottom, base came over the radio asking where I was. I asked them to give me a minute and explained the location he'd brought me to. As I was giving a description, Theo's line zipped out my hand and through bushes heading towards the main road.

I knew he'd found the burglars because of the speed at which he set off. The line burned my hand and I gave the command that I had a dog while I reined him back in. As Theo got closer, I could hear the burglars crashing through bushes and over fences. The second thought through my mind once I knew he was onto something was the fact that, for all his brilliance and talent, no police dog in the history of the force has ever had any road sense when they've got a scent. Theo was heading for a busy main road with a scent in his nostrils. Nothing could stop him except a car or truck travelling around 50mph.

I could hear the road was busy and despite screaming, 'No, no, no, no, NO!', I knew he wouldn't listen or even hear me over the roar of the cars. Fortunately, he made it across the road in one piece and I followed.

I couldn't see anyone disappearing, but Theo was up to a barbed-wire fence and, while desperate to get through and continue his chase, he'd got himself tangled up. A tangled-up police dog mid-chase is harder to undo than anything else in the world. He wouldn't keep still so it took me around thirty seconds to get him free to keep going.

I sent him on, but didn't realise I'd tangled his line around my leg so within seconds, I was pinned to the fence by my ankle, with Theo pulling and trapping me. As a handler, when you get into a tangle there's nothing worse and Theo knew he was onto something so wanted to keep going. He's strong and I was trapped so tight, I couldn't bring him back. He was whimpering to get on and keep going, but eventually listened and I could release myself.

We jumped over a wall and he made it to the end of the next field while I was still labouring through the one before. I jumped over another dry stone wall and landed in deep mud. As I went to move, one boot came off, but Theo was moving so fast, I didn't have time to put it back on again. I knew by the time I'd laced up, he'd be out of sight and I'd have no way of knowing which direction he'd gone in. As I followed suit, sprinting through mud with one boot on, I was cursing him.

He made his way into another farm and a courtyard. I could hear sirens and lights nearby and radioed to let everyone know Theo was off the lead so not to hare into the courtyard. When I made it to where Theo had been, he'd already disappeared into a paddock on the left. I could see him running up and down the same stretch, trying to figure out how to get through – there was a stile and he wasn't sure how to navigate it. I called him back, but he jumped the stile and I had no choice but to follow with one boot on. I was gaining on him when I heard a shout and I knew Theo had got them.

Within twenty seconds, I was on the scene. I remembered I was wearing the body camera as I was sprinting towards Theo; I was telling him I was coming and when

I got on the scene I called him off. On jobs like that, I always tell Theo I'm on my way, that I'm coming and almost there. Not for the assailants or the baddies, but for Theo – I want him to know I'm never far behind him.

Theo was exhausted but nothing like the two lads he'd caught. Beyond spent, their adrenaline had worn off. They weren't exactly physical specimens at the peak of fitness anyway and they were broken, muddied and desperate to rest. I wasn't much better than them – it had been a gruelling track over tough terrain, and I was bootless, breathless and broken.

'Two detained, I repeat, two detained ...'

After giving the shout back to the unit at the farm, arresting officers were on the scene in seconds. They'd followed at a safe distance and, as the two lads were carted off, I sat in the mud with Theo.

'You've done it, mate, you've done it! How? How on earth did you manage that? Every time I think I know you, every time I'm sure I've seen the best of you, you show me there's more.'

I checked him over to see if he was bloodied or bruised from the jumps and scrapes through barbed wire but there was nothing major. We'd started the track in daylight and now it was dark. As I hobbled back to the van, I saw a fellow handler who'd come on the shout to help if needed.

'You okay, G?'

Before I could answer, he was beside me, giving Theo a stroke.

'That will go down in history,' he marvelled. 'That's the most incredible track I'll ever bear witness to in my entire career.' He was saying what I was thinking: Theo had done everything perfectly. He'd been by the book, but had also shown that police dogs are thinking working animals who don't respond as computers do. It had all been caught on my body camera and the inspector had exactly what he wanted – a job from start to finish that showed what happens, what we come up against and how these fantastic creatures work with their human counterparts.

I got back to Hough End, wrote up the statement and handed in the footage. I was exhausted, but I knew I had to do it there and then in case I forgot anything with sleep.

The feedback from the top was that I'd done exactly what they wanted: I'd given them on a silver platter what they were after from body cam footage for dog handlers. It was described by the press as an 'epic police chase' and Theo was recognised for his bravery by the village, who presented him with a certificate.

The statement I wrote became the blueprint for national standards for new recruits. Claire was massively proud of both of us, and for weeks I had emails and congratulations from present and former colleagues, telling me what an amazing job I'd done. But it wasn't me, nothing is me.

It's Theo, he's the one who does it all.

15

WE WERE SIX WEEKS AWAY from Christmas 2016 and, while work was flying, at home Eryn and I became more of a team. I'd watch cartoons with her upstairs and not sit with Claire downstairs. Christmas came around again and Claire was on shift, while I got the house ready.

If I could pinpoint the exact time Claire and I started living separate lives, we probably could have or would have done something to address it. It felt like we'd come to a point in our lives where living like this felt normal.

Neither of us intended to end up where we were, that Christmas in 2016. We'd continue to wave to each other coming in and out of the work car park as I'd be coming off shift in the morning while she was coming on. We'd joke over Messenger that it was like we were separated, but neither of us made a single move to fix anything.

A few weeks after New Year, I was working a normal shift when we'd been called to look for a stolen car, a BMW. I raced to the scene with Theo. The police had given chase but the passenger of the stolen vehicle had stopped at lights and bricked the windows of the police car that was giving chase. At the next set of lights, the car had reversed and rammed the police car. They'd done some proper damage and the officers inside were injured but maintained pursuit until the vehicle was abandoned and the assailants made off on foot – that's when the shout came up for Theo and I.

By the time I arrived a few minutes later, they'd been on foot for ten minutes already. It was going to be tough, but I set Theo up and he pulled me straight into the woods. It was pitch-black. He identified a track and, within minutes, we'd been through woodland, onto road, around a reservoir and into more woodland. Theo couldn't find anything, so I decided to retrace our steps.

Neither of us was happy, but when a track didn't go how we wanted it to we'd quite often retrace and start again to see what else we could pick up. There was a helicopter overhead, which kept saying they had no heat signature (they weren't picking up anything that looked like suspects in the area) and they couldn't see anything. Comms were saying the same thing over the radio, but Theo and I weren't happy and we weren't giving up easily. We retraced and I told base not to worry about me, that I'd call if we needed anything or found anyone.

Everyone was wrapping up and I could hear the cars leaving.

Theo took me back to where we started the track and, instead of going right as he had, he went left. He waded into a swamp, the line was getting longer, and I followed him. I could tell by the time he'd tracked for a couple of minutes he was nailed on. We went over some conifers, through a stream, I struggled to scale a seven-foot fence, then we went through gardens. It was a physically tough track, but Theo would always get excited when he was nailed on. He'd try and jump a fence he couldn't and he'd whimper with excitement while I checked what was over the fence to make sure he didn't come to any harm when he scaled it in his usual effortless way.

After a few minutes in the pitch-black, we came out of one garden and there were wet footprints on the driveway. I called comms, who sent cars back, but as I did so Theo went into a bit of a panic. He stressed easily during a track, especially if he thought he'd lost the scent. With the cars yet to arrive, I pulled him back to me and gave him a fuss to calm him down.

'It's alright, Theo, don't worry. Just take it easy, son, okay?'

I pointed to the wet footprints and he inhaled really deeply. He reset and was off again. We went through a wrought-iron gate into another garden. I knew we were going to find them. I was trying to control my adrenaline, but Theo was getting pumped-up too. Theo took me to bins in an alcove, where he had a sniff but then went over a fence. He was still on his tracking line but the second he was over the fence it went like a fishing line and started whirring out of my hands.

I knew he was on it.

I knew we were going to be successful and I knew we'd find them.

I jumped over the fence, and Theo and the assailant were on top of a conservatory roof.

'6143, one detained!'

I gave the shout and Theo had yet again exceeded everyone's expectations. The episode epitomised his tenacity: everyone had given up, everyone had gone, but Theo hadn't.

The investigating DC was delighted with Theo and no one could believe what he'd done. I took him to the local petrol station for a cheese sandwich to celebrate.

Back at the station, the rest of the handlers were just

as delighted for him and for me. Dog handlers can wait their entire career for some of the jobs Theo was getting and now he was getting one after another, after another.

I wouldn't have changed anything at work that spring of 2017, but at home Claire and I were both skilled at putting things out of our heads and not confronting the elephant in the room, and for both of us work was a huge distraction. The intensity of every shift meant I didn't think about my marriage at all for around forty hours a week. It was a way of coping, but with hindsight a very bad one.

I tried to adjust to what my marriage had become but we were fast becoming different people. Both of us were at fault, none more than the other. I suggested counselling that spring and Claire agreed. We booked a session with a local counsellor and, fifteen minutes into the first session, she described our relationship as a war zone.

She was right. We didn't go back.

While Theo was thriving, so too was Sevvy: he'd located three bodies in eighteen months and recovered a piece of evidence that resulted in a murder conviction. I'd been party to internal meetings at work, where it had been suggested Theo could retire early – his service to GMP had been impeccable – and I'd work Sevvy as a body dog and take time off from the general dog-handling unit. It wasn't a proposition I'd jumped at to begin with. I loved working Sevvy, but shifts with Theo were adrenaline-packed and exhilarating.

Sevvy's jobs were emotionally gruelling. We'd spend days searching and, where Theo's success lay in catching a baddie and putting him in prison, success for Sevvy meant finding a dead body, someone's life extinguished, a future that would never happen.

It was always bittersweet when Sevvy was successful. He'd worked a few murders, including a four-day-old baby who'd been killed by his father. We successfully found the little lad who'd never get to grow up, but Sevvy's jobs were always incredibly tough emotionally. There was a huge satisfaction every time he did a good job, but when Sevvy found something it inevitably meant the worst had happened: someone was already dead. At least we could give closure to remaining family, but we couldn't avert disaster like Theo and I could and that took a big emotional toll on me. I'd become a police officer to help people and, while Sevvy was helping, I wanted to make things better and we couldn't. All we could do was try and bring peace to family members left behind.

Shifts with Sevvy would be days only, no nights. I'd have more time off and maybe I could sort the marriage and we could spend more time as a family. I'd also thought long and hard about retiring Theo myself. He was on such a fantastic streak, he'd made such a name for himself and was such an accomplished police dog, it felt like I wanted him to go out on a high. I wanted him retiring as a champion, not the washed-up boxer who stays in the game too long. No one but me had noticed any change in Theo – he was still as agile as he'd always been, but where before he could clear fences from standing still, now he'd have to take a run-up. He'd jump into the van at the start of every shift, but with not quite so much agility as he'd had when newly qualified.

It was selfish but I knew Theo would have a huge legacy and I wanted to protect it. For once at work it seemed like the powers that be and little me were on the same wavelength, though that wouldn't last long. I'd finished a meeting about it one shift in May 2017, when I got rumblings I might lose Sevvy.

To say my heart fell into my boots is an understatement.

He was wanted full-time in the search office because he was fast becoming the best nose on the body unit, but because I worked Theo too Sevvy couldn't do full-time. The inspector called to see me and I knew within seconds of setting foot in the office I was going to lose Sevvy. It

241

was implied the force was going to sell Theo and I had to choose between working Sevvy and losing Theo, or working Theo and losing Sevvy. I could have shouted loudly and pushed a computer off a desk, but I was older and wiser now and had seen more. There was nothing I could say or do that would change anything: I was too angry to cry, too resigned to fight.

'You're going to do what you're going to do, I'm going to work,' I said.

I knew I'd lose Sevvy and I was powerless. I adored that little Spaniel – he wasn't Theo, but he was a determined character, a gentle soul with so much fun in him. More than that, though, he was my dog. He was Eryn's dog too. I felt sick at the thought of having to explain to my daughter that her best friend, her little Sevvy, was leaving and would be going to another handler. He'd watch her go to school every day: he'd jump on top of the kennel in the garden and bark at her all the way down the road until she was out of sight. She'd spend the whole road looking back and waving at him, giggling at his tail making the whole back end of him shake with excitement. Similarly, when Sevvy was home and knew it was pick-up time, he'd sit on the top of the kennel watching and waiting for her face to appear round the corner at the end of the road. The second he could see her coming, he'd start barking and wagging his tail.

Eryn had raised him with me from a puppy: she'd trained him with me and they'd grown together. I knew she'd be broken-hearted at the thought of losing him, but she'd have been equally lost at the thought of losing Theo too. There was no way to win. All I could do was try to make it better for her as best I could.

Crushed, I walked out the office and made my way back to the kennels. In the relative privacy of my van with Theo in the back I cried like I'd cried when Denver died. I was a mess and still had hours to go on my shift when all I wanted was to be at home with Sevvy, Theo and Eryn.

I was trying to think about how to tell her when a shout came in. Jobs always took my mind off the tough stuff I was dealing with so I parked what I was feeling and switched on to work mode.

It was a pursuit of a burglary team off-road in a rural area.

I got to the scene and the helicopter was up and searching. The attending officer was at the point where the team had last been seen. I prepped Theo and we set off tracking. As usual, he took no prisoners and had me crawling through brambles in minutes. I was present in the job and gave 110 per cent, but all I could picture every time I blinked was Sevvy.

Theo had a scent but the helicopters couldn't see anything because the woodland was too dense. We got part way down a track and he stopped and took in a deep breath. He didn't move or motion to change direction so I pushed him on. We got to the end of the grove we were in and he stopped and looked back. He made it clear we'd gone wrong and I knew him well enough to know to take him back to the place he'd inhaled deeply.

We'd already been tracking for forty minutes and we were in an area you couldn't access, dense with brambles. We'd crossed a stream. Any other dog I'd have been sure it was a wild goose chase and would have insisted on taking them back to the van, but I trusted Theo implicitly. If he signalled to keep tracking, I'd follow as best I could.

We got to one area that was thicker and denser than anywhere else. The brambles were waist-high and there was no path. I unclipped him and he disappeared. Out of the corner of my eye, I saw a figure trying to crawl through the undergrowth. I issued challenges and Theo detained him. I signalled on the radio we had one detained and could hear the audible gasps on the radio and from the helicopter.

The manpower spent searching where Theo found him had been extensive. The helicopter had been out for the best part of an hour and despite having heat-seeking capabilities, I'd been told unequivocally there was no one in the woods and yet Theo had found him.

Sevvy waiting in the van dampened the usual elation I felt at Theo's success. I got back and, after checking Theo over to make sure he was okay, I took a picture of the two of them next to each other in the van. It wasn't something I usually did but because of the day I'd had and because their time together would be limited, I wanted to document it. I didn't know when I took it, but this would be the last time they were ever in a police van together.

I got home after the shift and sat Eryn down.

'You know Sevvy's so good and he's brilliant at his job?'

'Yeah, of course I do, Daddy. He's my dog, he's the best!'

She reached round his neck and gave him a squeeze. I took a deep breath and tried not to let my voice crack.

'Well, sweetheart, because Sevvy's so good at his job, he's been chosen for a very special role. He's the best because you trained him and he's been chosen for a very special job. But the thing about this job is that he won't be able to live with us anymore while he does it ...'

I looked up at the ceiling to stop the tears from falling and I could see Eryn doing the same thing. Biting her lip and trying not to cry, she nodded and hugged Sevvy even tighter. She didn't ask me any more questions and I left her and Sevvy to spend some time together.

Claire could see how hurt we both were. She adored Sevvy too and I could tell she felt helpless in the situation: she loved Eryn, she could see we were both hurting so much. She asked me why I wasn't fighting for him.

'The "G" I know wouldn't take it,' she implored me. 'He'd fight for him, he'd do whatever was needed. Where's your spark gone, Gareth? Don't let him go ...'

'I can't, Claire, I could lose my job. It's been decided and if I kick off and start making a huge fuss, I could be taken off the Dog Unit. It's happened before and I swore when I lost it the last time I'd never, ever do anything to jeopardise my position at work again. I can't win this one, I'm over a barrel. If I fight for Sevvy, I'll lose Theo. There's not a single thing I can do ...'

The following week, Sevvy was gone. I dropped him at the kennels and saying goodbye was one of the hardest things I'd ever had to do. He shouldn't have been going and there was an anger to my sorrow too, a powerlessness that I should have been able to prevent him going, but couldn't.

I was helpless.

After I managed to settle Eryn that night, I went to get Theo set for sleep. I fed him and put new bedding in his kennel. I could see he was restless but I knew I couldn't explain what had happened to him so I gave him a fuss and went into the house. For the next ninety minutes he howled and barked and whimpered. He was traumatised at losing Sevvy. I gave in eventually, brought him into the house and let him sleep in the utility room. His pack mate had gone and he couldn't understand what had happened.

Eryn spent the next few months drawing pictures of Sevvy and covering her room with them. She asked for the pictures of him as a puppy to be printed and framed for her room while I tried to carry on as much as I could as normal.

16

ERYN STRUGGLED MASSIVELY when Sevvy went and, while I tried to put on a brave face for her, I felt exactly the same. To make matters worse, he was still in Hough End so I'd see him every day and so would Theo. He'd start wagging his tail and Theo would stop to say hello every time we passed his kennel but I couldn't look at him. He wasn't my dog anymore and I respected the fact his new handler was trying to forge a relationship with him.

I felt myself physically tense every time I went by him when he was in the van, I missed him so much. All I wanted was to get in the kennel with him, bring Theo in and for the three of us to be back to normal, but I couldn't. He'd bark and bark at me when he'd see me and he'd whine for Theo, but there was nothing I could do. I also knew there were a lot of eyes on me seeing how I'd handle his transition so I couldn't let anyone see how upset, angry and broken I felt. I ignored him at work, he filled my mind and my heart at home, but I threw myself into work to compensate.

I was on a night shift in June 2017 when a shout came in – a car had been seen doing a drive-off (leaving a petrol station without paying). In isolation it wasn't much but comms said it had been doing jobs all day, drive-offs, causing disturbances; it had failed to stop when a patrol car tried to stop it too.

The job was in Hyde, and while Theo had been excelling at rural tracks I knew his urban search skills were just as strong. I gave him his usual pep talk in the back of the van. It was still strange, not giving Sevvy a stroke before closing him in and taking Theo, but I was trying my best to get used to the new arrangement.

Theo located the suspect almost instantly and I issued challenges, which were ignored. He latched on, but where suspects will usually yield, this lad wasn't going down without a fight.

There was a mate with him who wasn't getting involved at all – he was literally a bystander watching the whole thing unfold and offering support, encouragement and goading from the sidelines. He didn't seem a threat so I focused our efforts on the first lad.

Despite Theo having a grip of his arm, he'd managed to twist around and put Theo in a headlock. I'd never come across anyone treating my dog like that in all the years we'd worked together. It took me a few seconds to figure it out, but when I did I felt physically sick.

He was trying to break Theo's neck and he was a big strong lad who I guessed was capable of it.

My heart started pounding: this lad knew what he was doing and I was terrified something would happen to Theo. It wasn't like any other call-out we'd ever been on.

When Theo had been set on fire, I'd willingly chosen to use him as a sacrifice to potentially save the lives of other officers, but this was something different. This was a one-on-one, and where Theo had always succeeded he wasn't this time. I could hear him breathing heavily and I knew he felt exactly the same as I did. We were in new territory, both of us confused by what was happening and both wary and worried about how it was going to play out.

I kneed the lad in the face, hoping he'd release his grip on Theo enough that he could get away, adjust his bite and detain him once and for all. He was knocked off-balance and let go while he regained himself, giving Theo enough time to go in again. As Theo went in again on another grip, I heard the words I'll never forget: 'Bite him, George, bite his ear off!'

I was screaming and swearing at him to get off my dog; I was panicking, but all I could do was fight. I'd been a dog handler twelve years to that point but nothing, no training, can prepare you for that and no dog can be trained in how to react to that. Theo was experiencing something that had never happened to him before; he'd have been acting instinctively if he'd turned tail and run off but he wasn't going anywhere. Time stood still and, while my mind was blank and all I could do was fight, the one thing I kept thinking was that if Theo wasn't going anywhere, neither would I.

I'd never left his side and he'd never left mine.

The initial adrenaline rush of the fight started to wear off, but the lad we were fighting had taken something and was in another world. He was swinging and still trying to get Theo and bite him. Theo was anchored on, but with the suspect refusing to yield, he didn't know what to do next.

Things were going south pretty fast.

I heard him bite Theo, I heard the cartilage in Theo's ear go, so I put the lad in a headlock and tried to choke him out so he'd let go of my dog. There hadn't been any training for this – we hadn't been shown what to do or how to deal with someone trying to hurt our dogs when we'd been new recruits at Hough End – but here I was, with someone trying to hurt my dog and me fighting, brawling, to try and stay on my feet and save his life.

The lad let go of Theo, who rounded by my side and went to go in again. I was bent double with the lad in a headlock and all I could hear were horrendous thuds. It was like the sound of someone booting a football as hard as they could from zero range against a wall.

I lifted my head to see it was Theo who was being kicked repeatedly in the face. He was trying to get back in to anchor onto the suspect and detain him but every time he launched at him, this lad was kicking him as hard as he could in the face. The whole ordeal lasted over seven minutes and not once during that time did Theo give out so much as a whimper. He was bleeding, bitten and had endured more in those seven minutes than the entirety of the rest of his service yet unbowed, undeterred and unbroken, he kept on coming back.

In the melee, the lad had thrown my radio off me so I couldn't call for backup. I could see people recording the fight on their phones from their windows but no one was coming.

No help, no backup … It was me and Theo and I felt like we were fighting for our lives.

I managed to get the main suspect on the floor and his mate wasn't getting involved but was still shouting words of encouragement. Both Theo and I were exhausted and I knew the lad we were fighting was too because he'd wet himself. I didn't know what to do because it was something I hadn't been trained for. I wasn't sure whether to keep fighting, whether to call Theo off, whether to try and shout for help. It was bouncing around and we were all exhausted. If I could have stopped it and both of us gone our separate ways I would have but I'd never let anyone get away and I wasn't about to start now.

I could hear sirens coming from far away – someone who was filming had called the police – but they seemed to take forever to get to me. The second I saw the first van on the scene, I'd never been so happy.

The lad was detained and Theo and I made our way up the street and back to our van. A bobby I knew asked if I was okay. I didn't realise at the time both Theo and I were covered in blood but there was a huge sense of relief we were still alive. The lad had bust my lip wide open and it was pouring with blood. Theo had been kicked and bitten and was bleeding heavily too. I could see he was stressed and we were both in shock at what had happened.

That's the only job where Theo didn't win. He was used to winning every fight and hurting people with one bite. I'll never know what went through his head on that job and he'll never be able to tell me but I'll always be proud of the fact he didn't quit, he stayed toe-to-toe with me and stuck by me – his partner.

I gave Theo some water and checked him over. A handler mate came to check on us: Theo had chipped a tooth and was in a lot of pain. I could see he had bruising to his face and extensive bruising to his ribs because he'd shy away when I touched them and he couldn't lie down. I cleaned up my lip, packed Theo in the van and drove away from the worst job we'd ever been called to.

We drove for a few minutes to get out of Hyde and into the countryside. I knew we both needed medical attention but I wanted to try and process it together before I got us the help we needed. I let Theo out the van so he could do his business and while he limped gingerly onto the grass, I collapsed at the side of the van and cried like I hadn't done since I was a child.

For the first time ever, I was sick and tired of my job.

I was tired of missing Sevvy, tired of risking my life, tired of risking Theo's life. I wasn't paid enough to take the beating I'd just been given.

I was tired of hurting and tired of trying my best. No matter what we did, there were always more bad guys. We'd work relentlessly, we'd been partnered for years and yet the bad guys kept coming and they were getting more and more vicious. The cost to both Theo and I was starting to get too much.

As I replayed the fight in my head in slow motion, I felt sick when I recalled the lad trying to twist Theo's neck and snap it. Like he knew I needed something, Theo limped back to me gingerly and rested his head near me. I took a deep breath at the same time he did and stood up. Squaring my shoulders, I put him back in the van and drove to the station.

I got back to the nick and the sergeant told me they'd had a complaint from a member of the public about how I'd behaved. I'd expected it, but it still wasn't a nice feeling when I'd felt like I was in a fight for both mine and Theo's lives.

Theo didn't need stitches but he couldn't lie down for three days, the bruising was that extensive. He bounces back emotionally very well from the jobs where things don't go his way. Unlike humans, dogs don't overanalyse, or even analyse at all, so he's always been able to shake off the things that have happened to him.

My lip healed and, as a result of what happened to us, an element was added into training to teach recruits how to handle a situation similar to the one Theo and I had found ourselves in.

Within forty-eight hours of the incident, though, a video of the fight had found its way onto social media. I watched it and knew as a force we needed to get a handle on it. It was graphic and shot very close by. It was a dirty, horrible scrap and I felt queasy watching it – the sound of it bringing back horrible memories – but I also knew it was compelling to watch, that there'd be a lot of people who'd watch it.

I contacted the boss and let her know what had happened and that it was on social media. Within hours, all the national newspapers were trying to contact me directly and the Greater Manchester Police press office got involved and thankfully took over.

It had 500,000 views within twenty-four hours.

I'm never normally one to shy away from the spot-light – like *Send in the Dogs*, it's not unusual for me to court it – but the publicity from this was something I didn't want and didn't like. The video shows my dog being attacked and I couldn't protect him. Of all the jobs Theo had done where he'd thrived and succeeded beyond all odds, the one he was being propelled to fame for was one where we'd fared terribly. To this day I can't watch that video – for everyone who says how amazing Theo is in it, all I can see is my dog being hurt and I don't like it. Even if I could get it taken down, I wouldn't. I won't watch it, but it's an incredible example of what an amazing police dog Theo is.

While the public complaint was dismissed and the fanfare died away, Theo and I recovered and, after a few days off for him, we were back at the coalface.

In September 2017, Claire and I finally made efforts to save our relationship. We had a long talk when we found ourselves both off one Saturday afternoon. It was the most dialogue we'd had in months and each took a portion of the blame.

A week or so after our chat, I was called into the office at work and told I'd be getting a new pup. Theo was a year off retirement and the natural progression is that you faze one dog in and one out at the same time. You train your new pup and they also learn off your old one, but I wasn't sure how I felt about having a new dog.

Theo was a legend: it felt like I'd be betraying him by having another dog and working them instead of working him. How could I leave him at home and put another dog in the van? Besides, I knew no other dog would ever be as good. I'd been thinking long and hard about a change of pace, about hanging up my lead when Theo retired and moving on to a different branch of policing.

Claire didn't like me being a handler – she worried we'd get hurt or worse on a job. We'd seen some pretty bad things and had some very close scrapes so I couldn't help but think maybe it was time to try something else and accept the fact our luck wouldn't last forever. My marriage meant the world to me and the thought that a new job with better hours might give me my marriage back was a very tempting proposition. I had friends in other areas of the police who said they'd give me work if I wanted a new start. I was serious, but Claire saw through it and knew me better than I knew myself.

At the end of September, I got Mako, a German Shepherd. I brought him home from Wales where the force had chosen him, introduced him to Theo at eight weeks old and Theo took an instant dislike to him. He didn't like him and nothing I did could make them get on with each other.

I trained him on my own and he was doing okay but Theo refused to accept him. He'd snarl at him and growl every time they were anywhere near each other and where Sevvy had wormed his way into Theo's affections instantly, Mako didn't stand a chance: Theo didn't like him and he wasn't about to change. With hindsight, I didn't have the capacity to train him but, undeterred and unbowed, I continued with his training while working Theo.

I hadn't come to terms with the fact Mako's arrival meant Theo's retirement was edging ever closer and I should have dealt with that before I started trying to train a new dog. But I couldn't deal with the emotional fallout so I ignored a date I'd pretty much known would arrive when I first met Theo at Hough End and started training Mako.

That Christmas, we booked to go to Lapland. Eryn had wanted to go for ages and Claire and I decided to make the dream come true for her while she was still young enough to enjoy it all and believe. We'd taken Ben the first year we were together and wanted to do the same thing for Eryn. It was pricey but we reasoned that we'd worked hard and Eryn had been really good and deserved it.

Eryn was the perfect age to enjoy it, but Claire and I didn't talk much while we were there at all. Despite our long chat we'd both fallen back into the patterns of behaviour that had become habitual for both of us – co-existing under the same roof rather than being the couple we should have been. We needed the time away but it didn't go the way I wanted it to. I'd hoped removing the everyday stress would help us reconnect a bit, but it didn't.

Claire worked Christmas again and I got the house and the food ready.

We were back where we'd been months before.

Despite the state our relationship was in, we decided we'd visit my sister Suzanne in New Zealand in February 2018. We booked it before Christmas and we were going for three weeks of what was supposed to be sunshine and some family bonding. I hadn't seen my sister for seven years and, while we'd be staying with family, it was set to be the holiday of a lifetime and something we all desperately needed. Winter had been cold and work was miserable, so some beaches and sunshine would be exactly the tonic.

The kids were beside themselves with excitement. Eryn had never met Suzanne – only seen her on Skype and FaceTime – so she was excited to go and meet the cousins she didn't know she had and I was desperate to see my two nieces, who I'd last seen as babies.

We were travelling on 14 February in the evening from Manchester Airport, but a few hours before we were set to leave Claire's words ripped me in two.

'Gareth, I don't want to go. I don't want to go to New Zealand ...'

'Claire, we're supposed to be flying in a few hours ...'

I was so hurt, I wanted to cry. What sort of man was I, what sort of husband must I have been, who was so awful to be around my own wife didn't want to come on holiday or spend any time with me?

With some intervention from Claire's parents – she called them for advice – Claire agreed she'd come.

I dropped the dogs at the kennels, where they'd be looked after for the three weeks we were away, and the whole journey to the kennels and back, I couldn't help but wonder what state our relationship would be in afterwards.

From leaving in the taxi from home all the way to Dubai, Claire and I didn't utter a single word to each other. What we should have talked about was making the holiday the best it could be for the kids, having a final goodbye to each other and then splitting up when we got back.

We hadn't even touched down in New Zealand before I started longing to return home and get back to work.

Theo was my constant when things were rough. Here I was, in New Zealand with things as bad as they could be, and he was halfway round the other side of the world.

My brother-in-law picked us up from the airport and, with Suzanne and him around, our problems were diluted for a while. The kids had a fantastic first few days, but before the end of the first week my sister pulled me aside.

Claire had spoken to her about how unhappy she was. She'd told Suzanne she hated the way I dressed and hated my teeth. It all felt so superficial yet so unbelievably wounding at the same time. I hadn't changed physically since we met but, rather than focus on the big emotional issues in our marriage, Claire had found fault with how I looked and the fact I'd never had braces fitted to fix my wonky teeth. Suzanne was worried sick about me and had been hurt by the comments too.

It was my birthday forty-eight hours later and we were supposed to be going out for a family meal. My brother-in-law asked us all to pose for a photo and I flatly refused – I didn't care that it made the whole meal awkward, I was done.

We had a conversation that night where I asked Claire if she wanted to be with me. She said no and, like that, it was over – the marriage I'd thought would last forever finished in one word. I've never been so lonely as I was those three weeks – I was never alone but it was the loneliest I'd ever felt. I'd left home a married man and came back from New Zealand knowing my marriage was done.

17

I HEADED STRAIGHT TO THE KENNELS to get Theo the second we got back. He was exactly the tonic I needed. He was more excited to see Eryn than me but my unit, my pack, were back together again.

Within days of coming back, Mako was ditched from the unit. His training had been going well but he wouldn't bite. I could have trained him if he'd been my only priority, but he wasn't. He wouldn't play, which signified he had no prey drive – it's the instinct all dogs should have to pursue and capture prey, and it's what we use when training them to bite. That and the fact Theo refused to accept him. I knew life would get harder once Theo retired and Mako started working. I'd focused on training him well, but my heart hadn't been in it as it had with Theo and, while I adored him, I knew deep down Mako had come along at the wrong time and would be better off as a pet than someone's police dog.

With Mako gone, it was made clear at work in no uncertain terms that I'd have to find another police dog to train. Theo's retirement was getting closer every day and, when he retired, I had to have a fully trained police dog ready to step up and take his place.

With my marriage over, I relied on Theo more than ever. I knew Claire and I were over, we both did, but moving out wasn't an option for me. I had a Greater Manchester Police dog and there are certain legal issues that go along with working with one: they must have a proper structured kennel and run at your home property.

I couldn't move Theo's kennel and so I couldn't move out.

I slept on the sofa while Claire stayed in our room. We started living separate lives again and I threw myself into work mode. The kids didn't notice I was sleeping downstairs because I was always in bed after them and up before them.

Plenty of the jobs I do shift-to-shift are instant call-ins but, every now and then, there's a known person or gang who are repeat offenders.

Just over six months after Theo had been bitten, and days after getting back from New Zealand, we had a call to a burglary. Intelligence suggested there was a team operating and they had a very specific method or signature for breaking into properties. Theo and I had been alerted to an abandoned car, which had been stolen in a burglary the previous night. We drove onto the street and, rather than just find the stolen vehicle, there were two more and each car had men outside it.

We'd found the team behind the burglaries swapping cars, all of which were stolen. It was a golden opportunity but they'd seen us just as we'd seen them and the men were all getting into cars with the clear intention of driving off and not giving up.

Theo and I jumped out and I grabbed the driver's door of one car before the lad in it had a chance to close it. The driver slammed it into reverse, took out the other two cars, sending one careering into a garden on the street and another into the other side of the road. He was reversing while I was hanging onto the car door and I was convinced my number was up.

Weighing up my options, I decided that I had no choice but to hold on. The door was open and I didn't even need to issue a command to Theo – he jumped through the door and latched onto the driver's arm, which was on the steering wheel.

I've never seen Theo do such a fantastic bite: he was so clean and precise with it, the guy who was driving seized up and took his feet off the pedals – which was enough for the car to lose momentum and stall, and for me to drag him out.

Theo had been successful and we'd done it again, but looking at the scene it was utter carnage. There was a car in a garden, cops all over the place, police cars and vans. It definitely wasn't covert as operations go but the job was done and Theo had averted disaster and saved the day yet again.

After I called Theo off and took him back to the van, I appraised what had happened. If it wasn't for his quick thinking, I'd have been run over. It's happened to police officers before – PC Gareth Phillips was left with life-changing injuries in August 2018 after being mown down by a car and PC Andrew Harper was killed a year later, in August 2019, after being run over while attempting an arrest. We know as officers what our job entails but, when facing the prospect of death in the line of duty, it takes you a while to process it. If it wasn't for Theo, I could have died or been left with life-changing injuries.

I went to the hospital afterwards to check on the prisoner. He complained and claimed Theo had been on him, biting him for fifteen minutes, but, thanks to the body cam footage that had become the norm, Theo was exonerated because it showed he bit him for four seconds – four valuable seconds that saved my life. It's easy to think I'd be raging with what he was claiming, but I learned a long time ago that criminals don't operate by the same levels of honesty and fairness as the rest of the population. There is no honour among thieves. None.

That job affected me more than I cared to admit at the time. It was the closest I'd ever come to losing my own life in the line of duty but it was also the only job we've ever done where Theo took the lead and acted on initiative. In that moment when the car started to drag me, I couldn't have issued a command if I'd wanted to. Theo assessed the situation and had my back. More than a police dog, he was an equal: he was my partner and he protected me like any partner on two legs would have done.

I went home that night and kissed Eryn while she slept and checked on Ben. Claire was watching TV, and while I wanted to sit down and tell her everything something stopped me. Would she be mad that I risked my life that way? I was a father after all, but Eryn and Ben hadn't even come into my head when I grabbed the door – I'd acted instinctively and done my job. I don't know what

Claire would have said or thought, though, because I didn't tell her. She could have been the support I so desperately needed that night even though we were over, but I didn't give her the chance to show me. Instead I made myself a cuppa and went out to Theo and sat with him while I came to terms with it.

Over the next few days and weeks I found myself thanking him a lot. He'd never grasp what he'd done, but I'll never forget it.

That burglary job felt like a sea change. When I was first handed a job on the Dog Unit, I thought all my dreams had come true. Don't get me wrong, I still loved my job, but I was getting sick and tired of risking mine and Theo's lives. We'd been lucky so far, but when might that luck run out? It felt like the jobs were getting more dangerous, the recovery times when things went wrong taking longer too. We'd done everything by the book and I'd gone above and beyond in the line of duty yet still I'd lost Sevvy, still I was risking Theo.

I was growing sick of being a dog handler and I never thought I'd feel that way. It unhinged me a bit – it had been my sole purpose since childhood and after thirteen years, it was tough to admit there were huge parts of it I didn't love as much as I had done when I was newly qualified. I was privileged to have the job, I knew that, but it felt like we'd gone from routine jobs to jobs that cost us dearly, emotionally or physically.

Were we getting better at our jobs and so the risk level was higher or were crimes getting tougher?

The victories we'd enjoyed in our early days together were still there and were still plentiful, we were the successful team we'd always been but those victories were now coming at a cost: neither of us was unscathed by what we were dealing with, Theo physically and me emotionally. Friends on the Dog Unit were noticing it too but I couldn't give it up, it was all I'd wanted to do and it felt like all I knew how to do, so Theo and I did what we do best: we kept going and we kept catching baddies.

Theo was nominated for the *Sun*'s Hero Dog awards in April 2018 and was a runner-up. He'd spent the day in London being fussed by presenter Christine Lampard and it was a lovely distraction.

We had a family holiday with friends to Turkey planned in the May of 2018 and, while I'd refused to go initially, Eryn persuaded me to change my mind. Claire and I were on speaking terms and the fallout from New Zealand had thawed. The anger and resentment we'd both felt had given way to the day-to-day job of holding down work and parenting kids – we had to organise Ben and Eryn and their school and club commitments – but our chats didn't go past that.

It wasn't so much thought of as a last-ditch effort to save anything, but Claire sent me a message saying we'd paid for the holiday, there were other people who were counting on us being there and we could exist separately yet still give the kids a good time.

The kids had a good time and I focused on them.

When we got back later that month, I got wind of a dog, a fourteen-month-old juvenile, who immediately piqued my interest. A friend in the South Yorkshire force Dog Unit had told me about a Belgian Shepherd Malinois they were selling. I knew I'd have to replace Mako and the powers that be would start breathing down my neck unless I did so soon.

Malinois are incredibly smart and obedient dogs but they're very protective and very territorial too. On paper, they're all the ingredients for a perfect police dog but trained badly or not socialised enough, they can be a loose cannon with a set of very strong jaws. We hadn't had one in Greater Manchester Police for more than a decade and, as I needed a distraction or a new challenge, I wanted to be the first person to have one.

I wanted something in my next dog that would set me apart from everyone else. I couldn't replace Theo – I knew I couldn't – but what I could do was have an entirely new breed, something entirely different, a new dog, not one who I'd constantly compare to Theo.

I went straight to my boss with the proposition and, as expected, I was told in no uncertain terms that the Dog Unit under no circumstances would ever have a Malinois in its kennels. Rather than move on, though, I dug my heels in. I wanted this pup and something inside told me pursuing it and not taking no for an answer was the right thing to do.

Getting Kai became my focus and, six weeks later, I brought him home. It was 12 June 2018, and as much as I hated the thought of Theo retiring, I knew Kai was the right dog to step into his lead when the time came. It felt right to get a new breed too – I didn't want another Shepherd because none would compare to Theo so a Malinois seemed appropriate, respectful and right.

A clean sweep and a new start rather than a replacement.

Theo came with me to pick him up because I wanted them to meet each other instantly …

Kai was fourteen months old when Theo first laid eyes on him. He wasn't a puppy like Sevvy had been, but Theo instantly accepted him, which was a huge relief. Kai was happy to be subservient to Theo – something I think helped to secure their bond – and it felt like Theo had appraised him and deemed him good enough for me. It was as if Theo could sense what was happening and where he'd felt Mako wouldn't serve me well as a police dog, he seemed to feel Kai was good enough – that Kai was up to the job of being my partner, walking in Theo's pawprints.

18

THEO WAS SET TO RETIRE in March 2019 so I had nine months to make Kai into the police dog Theo was. He was a specimen, an absolutely beautiful-looking dog. He was tall and long-limbed; you could see from him standing or sitting he'd be incredibly agile and, when I took him to work to show him off, he was the envy of all the handlers.

I unclipped him to start some gentle training, though, and he ran off. I'd wondered why South Yorks were getting rid of Kai and right there, with a bushy tail disappearing round a tree, was my answer. His recall left a lot to be desired and, suddenly, a nine-month time frame felt very short.

Theo was still working as hard as ever and I was determined his last year of service would be his best. We had in excess of twenty bites in 2018 – that's twenty successful jobs, a great ratio for any police dog.

In June 2018, the same month I got Kai, we were sent to Bolton on a specific operation: an area was getting hammered for burglaries and they wanted to see if Theo could track the assailants after one. It was a team and we knew the vehicle they were using. Because of the state of things at home, I jumped at the chance of a weekend job away. It was set to be a Friday to Sunday, but within two hours of starting on the Friday, I ended up behind the car in question.

There was a chase before the driver abandoned the vehicle. After challenges, I sent Theo in and he detained him. What was expected to be an all-weekend job was wrapped within a few hours of starting, thanks to Theo.

While I'd come home from shifts and Eryn would ask me excitedly how many baddies Theo had caught, she still longed for Sevvy. She'd draw pictures of us as a family, but Sevvy would always be beside her. She'd talk about him all the time.

Losing him changed her. For the first time she had to grow up a little and, as a father, for me that was heart-breaking. I'd always been able to make things better, soothe her, but I couldn't fix the hole Sevvy had left in her heart. I'd focus on Theo and tell her how great he'd done and, while she was always proud and fussed him, I could see constantly how much she missed that little Spaniel.

The following month, we came on duty: there'd been a team on mopeds who'd committed nineteen robberies the same day. They were nasty, violent robberies and, while we'd witnessed a rise in moped crimes, this was something we hadn't predicted and didn't see coming.

I had a recruit with me who was shadowing us because he wanted to be a handler. We were midway through a briefing when firearms piped up over the radio that they were behind one of the suspected mopeds and criminals. They followed them to a derelict industrial area, but it was massive and they lost sight of them just as Theo and I turned up with our new recruit.

There were two lads who'd made off and the search began in an old brick factory area of the estate. We searched the whole area and, on the very last compound we checked, I sent Theo off to search.

I was chatting to the recruit about what we'd done and how you need to section a search area that size to make sure you strategically cover all of it when I stopped dead.

I saw Theo change and I knew he had a scent.

Those moments are always the most perfect of a dog-handler's career. I loved watching Theo get a scent.

277

That recognition, knowing I could read his body language, it always gives you a shiver of excitement. It had started off as a job I didn't expect much from – by the time we got on scene there'd been other dogs and police that had searched the area – but because it was a good show of what Theo could do, I'd continued with the search to show the new recruit.

I didn't expect him to turn anything up, but I realised straight away I'd underestimated Theo's nose and tenacity. He stopped still at a concrete brick wall. It was about 30 feet up and I knew instantly there was someone behind the wall, which was in between two buildings. I shouted the challenges before climbing up myself and seeing a lad cowered and tucked in the corner. Everyone else had searched exactly the same area and had come away, sure there was no one there.

Theo had scented the lad from around half a mile away, diligently followed his instincts and ensured an arrest. Theo overwhelmed the recruit I was with – anyone else might have put him back in the van, given him a treat and headed off into the sunset, but I knew if Theo had found one, the chances were the other lad would be here too.

I put him back on his long line and we went back to the beginning.

The helicopter was up and, despite Theo wanting to head left, the eyes in the sky told us to head right – they had a heat source so, while I moved us right, Theo kept looking left. Within a few seconds, the heat source made itself known to be a big fat tabby cat. Theo looked distinctly unimpressed at a helicopter impeding his nose so I let out some line and let him do things his way.

We'd been searching for around forty-five minutes when Theo needed the toilet. He was mid-business at the edge of a raised platform we were searching when he looked over the edge and disappeared: he'd found the other lad in question without even trying too hard.

The pair of them were convicted of all nineteen robberies.

That summer was a long, hot one. While I love my job at any time of year, a track in the freezing cold in the dead of night is always exhilarating. Dragging yourself in uniform when the warm summer nights are close with no movement is always more exhausting for both handler and dog.

In August, there was a report of a stolen vehicle on different plates armed with a shotgun. After a pursuit with a police car, they crashed their vehicle and made off into a park in Stockport. Theo and I were called, but were by no means the first on the scene.

I took him to the top of the park, where a police officer briefed us. It was unknown whether they had a shotgun but they'd run off into the woods. I was told I didn't have to go in as there was a risk they had a gun, but Theo looked at me in such a way I had no choice.

I put him on a long line and he set off. As he headed through the trees and down a steep slope, I struggled to keep up. He took a right and we were on the edge of a riverbank. He dived left and detained a lad I hadn't even seen. We brought him out and, thankfully, he didn't have a shotgun.

Then there was a stolen vehicle job in August, where Theo received a commendation from the prosecuting QC. He said in his closing statement we were a credit to the force and called for us to be honoured by the chief constable.

In Theo's final year of service, the jobs were coming thick and fast and he was acing them all.

In October, we were called to search for a wanted male who had been missing for weeks. I was asked to concentrate on it for a day and see what I could do – I had an area and vague vehicle description.

We got to the area we were supposed to search in and, as luck would have it, a car passed me, matching the description of the vehicle. We ended up in pursuit and he ditched the car and legged it into the woods.

I put Theo on his line and together we set off into the woods, not far behind him. Within seconds, Theo had pulled me to a riverbank and then into the cold river after the lad. Completely out of my depth, I was being swept downstream. There couldn't have been a more inopportune time but comms came on my radio asking for an update. I didn't want to say I was soaking and floating away so I asked for a minute to update them.

Theo's such a strong swimmer, for him it was a normal part of a pursuit but I was scrambling to get back onto the riverbank and follow on land while he swam. The radio went again requesting an update and this time I was honest: 'I'm in a river in the middle of nowhere, I'm freezing and I'm trying to find him. Will you all bloody hold on?'

Theo tracked him out the river through the woods and found him on the roadside, sopping wet and shivering. It took me forever to warm up and I had a go at Theo for dragging me in, but I couldn't help but see the funny side when we got back to the kennels and everyone was ribbing me about our swim.

That same month, Claire moved back into her mum's house with Ben. It made sense for her to move so the dogs could stay settled. We'd share Eryn, who loved staying with her grandparents anyway. It was an attempt for us to see whether some space away from each other might work things out. We'd agreed to separate and see what happened rather than split up for good immediately. We both agreed to it because we had Eryn and Ben, and the least they deserved was for us to give things a go if we possibly could. Neither of us was under any illusions but we'd give separation a try.

I knew we needed space too if we were to have a hope of reconciling. I don't think many couples split with the thought of ending it initially and, although my marriage for the last year had felt like death by a thousand paper cuts, I wanted to breathe a little and get some perspective. We knew we owed that to Eryn and to Ben to try one more time before giving up on us completely. Besides, I'd spent so many hours thinking and fretting about my relationship, I wanted some time and some space to think about nothing.

My focus – possibly to the detriment of my marriage – has always been my job. After the river dip in October, I learned that Kai would shortly be starting a six-week course to qualify as a police dog. He'd pass out in December and Theo's last shift would be on 30 November 2018.

I had just months to make Kai into the police dog he should be and just weeks left of working with Theo. It would fly by and I wanted to make sure I focused on every single shift. I knew the memories I'd made with Theo would have to last me a lifetime and I had to make sure I drank in every last moment, every last search, every last pursuit and track.

Ben knew what was happening at home: he was sixteen and a smart kid. He'd seen it coming and, while I told him he could ask me anything and that I was there if he needed anything, he processed it on his own like I knew he would. Claire had spoken to Eryn, telling her Mummy and Daddy were taking a break and were going to be friends for a while.

I threw myself into work and the kids and prayed time would slow down.

On 19 November, though, time stood still for all the wrong reasons.

A colleague on the dog-handling unit nearly lost his life when he got out of his car to pursue an assailant on foot, only to be chased by another car. I was in the vehicle behind him and watched it all unfold. He'd followed the car down a dead-end street and tried to box it in. He was out of his vehicle and trying to smash the window to get in, but the car reversed back and I could see it was going to squeeze through the gap, which would pin him against the wall. I screamed over the radio for him to get out the way and he dived to the side a split second before a car travelling around 40mph would have hit him.

You're trained never to use your car to shunt another vehicle unless you absolutely have to, but I made the split-second decision that the only way I was stopping the car was to use my vehicle to shunt it. The driver had nearly killed Lee, who had listened to me and jumped out the way. If we continued the high-speed pursuit, it could be a member of the general public next, who wouldn't have a radio on and wouldn't hear me shout to get out the way.

When it happens on shift an officer is called out and the whole thing has to be documented there and then. It's called a PVA – a Police Vehicle Accident – and it's not something you do lightly. I managed to shunt it, sending it spiralling out of control before coming to a standstill. Where I'd managed to get the outcome I wanted, it was at a huge cost – I'd written off eight cars on the street and damaged a further eight too. It was far from ideal but I had no choice. I'd used my vehicle to make sure Lee was safe and out of danger and to ensure no one else was killed.

It was one of the most heart-stopping moments of my career. Seeing that vehicle racing towards Lee is an image

I'll never forget. Lee's dog Sky had run off and the whole dog team searched for her until we found her a while later. She was okay, but had high-tailed it away as a self-preservation instinct. My life at home and my real family might be falling apart but that night I was able to make sure my work family, all two-legged ones and all four-legged ones, were safe and well.

As Theo's last shift drew ever closer, I was pleased with the progress Kai was making, and I spent more and more time trying to get my head around what it would be like working another dog. The relationship Theo and I had was so instinctive, I knew he had my back. I didn't know that yet about Kai and I'd have to keep reminding myself I'd have to switch on and not leave anything to chance when we started working together.

Theo hadn't started his working life as the most incredible police dog I'd ever worked and arguably the most successful in Greater Manchester Police. He'd become that dog little by little, job by job and shift by shift. I couldn't presume anything about Kai when we started working together. I'd have to go back to being the handler I was when I started working Theo and I'd need to be patient and let time and experience work their magic on Kai as they had done on Theo.

19

IF I COULD HAVE GOT TIME to stand still, I would have done. If I'd have been able to go back to the start of Theo's working life and relive every job again, I'd have jumped at the chance but, as sure as night follows day, inevitably the date I'd circled on the calendar at home rolled around.

Nothing I could do would slow it down. It was Theo's final shift and, after eight more hours of service, the life he'd dedicated to Greater Manchester Police would be his own again. No more 'thieves on', no more issuing commands, no more 'seek on'. He'd always been my dog, but in eight hours he'd be my pet.

It was with a heavy heart that I dressed and called him up into the van for the last time. We'd been working all week in countdown and, as usual, Theo had been brilliant and assisted two arrests. We were both tired but I was emotionally drained too. I'd taken in cakes for everyone at the kennels as per the tradition on your dog's last shift and the whole atmosphere at work was a sad one. Changing dogs and retiring one you've worked with is part of the job. You're told that from the very beginning, but every handler on the unit feels a sadness when one dog goes and another one starts.

Theo had been a legend: every single dog handler loved him and they were all sad to see him go. I'd managed to rub a few people up the wrong way but Theo was adored across the board. I'd spent thousands of hours policing with him and always talked to him about everything. He listened as only dogs can and I'd spent weeks in the run-up telling him we were heading towards his final shift. Of course, he didn't know he wouldn't be coming with me in the van anymore – he had no idea this shift was different to any other and that broke my heart. I couldn't explain the gravitas of the night for him and I couldn't stop his confusion that would be inevitable when I next went on shift with Kai and didn't take him too.

I'd always said if Theo could talk and drive I'd be out of a job. It's not the size of the dog in the fight, it's the size of the fight in the dog. Theo was never a natural police dog, he just developed like me and together we were unstoppable. He sustained so many injuries that should have had him turning tail and running away but every single minute of every shift he was right by my side. The only time he ran off was to put himself out when he was on fire and even then he was back inside twenty seconds, singed and in pain but ready to go toe-to-toe with whoever he needed to.

Our last shift was a quiet one – we hadn't done much and it got to 4.20 a.m. with us set to finish at 5 a.m. I wanted one last job, one last search. I parked us up on a quiet road and got Theo out the van. After taking his picture by the van, I posted it on Instagram.

At 4.30 a.m. I posted:

Well, that's it, Manpol Theo has completed his last shift as my faithful partner. 4.30 a.m. and a slight tear. This dog from nervous unassuming soul that he was has developed into what I can only describe as the best police dog I've ever had the pleasure to work or witness. He's been a credit to GMP and saved me and people dear to me on more than one occasion. Many jobs hold memories. I've seen him kicked, punched, bitten and set on fire and he's always stayed true. Of all the jobs, one stands out and I will be forever grateful for what he did that

night. Thank you, son, time for me to look after
you now. xx

Having posted it, I was crying hard. I sat Theo back in
the front seat and we shared a cheese sandwich while I
chatted to him.

'I couldn't ask for any more from you, son. You've
done everything I've asked and more, and I want to say
thank you. I also want to say sorry for all the times I've
wronged you. I'm sorry I've lost my temper with you
and I'm sorry I've shouted at you. We've been through
so much, haven't we? What will I do without you? Will
you ever settle down and be happy not working?'

We sat chatting for twenty minutes until our shift
finished. I put him in the back again, gave him a pat and
shut the sliding door. I drove back to the nick with a
lump in my throat. I'd been crying and I knew everyone
at work would see that, but I didn't care – Theo was my
world and our dream team was ending that night. We'd
never work together again, our last shift had been a
quiet one.

When I got to the junction to turn right into the
kennels I decided to do one more loop, one final drive
round with my partner. I was feeling nostalgic and
emotional when over the crest of the hill came a set of

headlights moving far too fast: it was a white car going around 120mph.

'6143, urgent!' I shouted over the radio. I could hear the respondent on the other end, 'Oh heck …'

Everyone knew it was Theo's last night and they all knew I'd wanted him to go out on a high. If I'd taken that turn when I should, we'd be back in the kennels with tea and cake. Instead we were in a high-speed pursuit of what I guessed to be a stolen vehicle.

The majority of the force was getting ready to sign off night shift. There were handlers and PCs all in the nick waiting to celebrate Theo's last shift and expecting him to come through the door. Rather than tea and cake, though, they dashed out to their cars and started after us.

The car went into the estate where I used to live – the one I'd grown up in – and I knew it couldn't get out. There was one road in and the same one out. I got to where I knew it would be. It flashed by me and I started pursuing.

The chase went on, but no one was giving up.

The helicopter was out too.

I was trying to stay calm, but I knew I wanted Theo to get these guys more than anything in the world.

The car team had stung the vehicle so it was running on flat tyres. Theo knew we were onto something and, when the car pulled up and the guys inside fled, we were one of the first vehicles on the scene.

The police who'd got there before us pointed in the direction where the driver and passenger had fled. They'd gone over walls and so I sent Theo after them. He cleared the walls with room to spare and disappeared into the darkness as I issued challenges.

I heard he'd held someone and I followed to make the arrest. We knew there were another two who'd absconded, though, so Theo and I continued our search while one was taken into custody. I heard over the radio another handler had detained one of the other assailants, which meant there was one more to find.

We got into the eighth garden down from the initial find and Theo ran past a shed door but doubled back in a split second. He went into the shed and, within seconds, he'd pulled another one out and I was able to radio we'd detained the final guy. We had all three of them lined up and everyone burst into a round of spontaneous applause for Theo. The shift was ended, and he'd spent his final minutes doing what he did best.

I'd had such a shot of adrenaline while the job had been going on and I'd been feeling hugely emotional before we started the pursuit. It was like Theo knew it was his last job after we'd had a chat in the van. Like he got the gravitas that we'd never be together in a working capacity again so he gave everything he had for that last job. I'd have searched all night for them because I wanted to give Theo one last shot, one last job where he could do what he does best and go out on a high.

I was suddenly exhausted and completely bereft all at the same time. Through everything, Theo had been my true north – the one compass point in my life I could always navigate by. We'd spent thousands of hours together: he was my protector, my partner, my colleague, my friend and way more than just my dog. Even though this moment had been a year in the making – hell, I'd known when Theo was training he'd retire at eight and a half, like all police dogs do – I was suddenly so rudderless and so terrified of what the future held without him.

Back at the nick, the other handlers all took their time to fuss Theo and give him a treat. He loved each and every one of them and, as was tradition, he was made a proper fuss of.

The fast vehicle response drivers had come by the kennels too – Theo had worked with a lot of them and they'd made sure they put their heads in to give him a fuss too. Theo was a legend on the force: everyone who worked with him remembered him and, as with any other colleague, they wanted to show their respect, reverence and thanks.

I got home after everyone had said their goodbyes, put Theo to bed and gave him the longest fuss, kissing his head where I'd kissed him thousands of times before. He didn't know we wouldn't be going back out again in the morning or the next night so he padded into his kennel and lay down to sleep.

It was a hugely special night for me but I was home alone with no one to share it. I tried to sleep, but tossed and turned, wondering what was to come next. I'd relied on Theo for so much for the last eight years. He'd saved my life, given me my career, helped me through heartache and pain; he'd listened when no one else would. I knew he was still mine and he wasn't going anywhere but how would things change?

Would they change at all, or was I being paranoid?

I spent the next few days mulling over some of Theo's biggest and best jobs. They were so vast, so different, his expertise and his skill level utterly unrivalled. I'd been the one to get the credit for all his work – okay, I'd always treated him to cheese sandwiches – but the only reason I was one of the most respected dog handlers in Greater Manchester Police was because of Theo's success.

What would happen to me, to my career, if Kai didn't step into the breach?

I couldn't imagine going to work without Theo. Of course, I still had Kai, but the thought of putting a different dog in the van and working Kai wasn't something that filled me with excitement.

It was like I'd lost an arm.

Over the coming days, I continued training Kai, but I'd sneak Theo into work because I couldn't bear to leave him at home. I'd bring him with me and leave him in the kennels because it felt wrong not having him with me. It was selfish and it must have been confusing for him but I felt like I was starting to unravel, and I knew when Theo was around I didn't feel like that.

I should have sought help, should have spoken to someone, but Theo was the band-aid I needed and I kept him near me as a way of coping. I did a good job of hiding how I was feeling from everyone, even the close friends on the Dog Unit I'd made over the years. I didn't know what I'd have said even if someone noticed – 'I'm not coping, but Theo makes me feel like I can keep going'? We all love dogs on the unit, it's why we do what we do, but I knew my need for Theo would have raised a few eyebrows if I'd mentioned it.

* * *

Two weeks after Theo's last shift, I moved out of the house Claire and I had bought as our family home. We'd decided to sell it and split for good. Sixteen hours after it went on the market in October 2018, it had sold and we had to clear everything out by the middle of December.

I was house hunting and had to find a place I could put a kennel in. Try as I might, none of the gardens I was looking at were big enough for a kennel for two police dogs. I was training Kai, sneaking Theo into work too and wondering what my career would look like without him in it. It was one of the most stressful times of my life at a pretty stressful time of year when everything seems to be about love and families and time together. Inevitably, something was going to snap at some point.

By the start of December, I still hadn't found a house and had nowhere to go. I had no choice but to put my dogs into kennels. I spoke to the unit and explained the situation I was in – I didn't know how long the dogs would be in and vowed I'd spend my weekends training them and taking them out. With them housed and all my belongings in storage, I started living in my car.

I'd gone from having it all – a relationship, a house, a family, a career – to being alone without a roof over my head and an unknown career in front of me. The confidence I'd enjoyed professionally until that point had dwindled and I realised almost all of it had come from Theo. Colleagues and bosses thought I was a great handler, but the only reason I'd been great, the only reason I'd been a success, was because of Theo. He defined me, he was me, and I couldn't work him ever again. Who would I be without him? I had no idea and was scared to find out.

I started drinking – just a glass or two of red wine to begin with, then a bottle. Anything to take my mind off my life when I wasn't working. I'd have wine and text Claire, asking if we'd done the wrong thing, I'd tell her how much I loved her. Understandably, she didn't want drunken late texts from me and told me as much.

On Christmas Day 2018, I got drunk at a friend's house – we were going through the same thing so started drinking early and fell asleep early too.

I spent Boxing Day with Eryn – we went straight to the kennels and spent the day with the dogs. We played on the field for hours and then I took her for dinner and to the cinema before I dropped her back to Claire. Afterwards I parked back in the kennels and spent Boxing Day night in the car with Theo.

Between Christmas and New Year, I stayed with friends here and there, and ringing in 2019 with Eryn at the Horse of the Year show in Liverpool I wondered what the year had in store for me. I'd spent last New Year with my family in my own home and somehow in the last 365 days it had all unravelled. I had Eryn and the show was a Christmas present – she loves horses almost as much as she loves dogs – but we didn't have our own home to go back to anymore and that hurt.

In January, I returned to work, trying to stay positive. I'd had a terrible festive season but I was doing my best to see the New Year as a new opportunity. I wasn't paying a mortgage so I moved into the local Travelodge – at least I had somewhere to retreat to and, while I didn't have the dogs with me, I was spending time with them after work in the kennels and out on long walks before I'd take them back and go to the hotel to sleep.

Kai passed out with flying colours the first week of January. His training had been textbook and, while I'd still been house hunting over Christmas, I'd found the perfect little house with a garden for the dog kennels and a lovely bedroom for Eryn. I could move in on 21 January. It was the good news I needed and it felt like I'd finally rid myself of any festive negativity.

The house was what you might call a 'doer-upper' but, the second I'd set foot inside and had a look around, I knew it would be perfect. I instantly pictured Eryn hopping down the stairs on Christmas morning before I saw any of the other rooms. It felt right, it felt like home, and when I got the keys it felt like everything was starting to come together again. I got Theo and Kai, and we spent the first night on the floor together.

Claire and I had established a dialogue through text. Time apart had served us both well and, because we'd continued communicating through text about the kids, we'd become a little chattier.

A month after I moved in, I learned from mutual friends that Claire had met someone else and been on a couple of dates. We didn't owe each other anything, we'd split up, but my stomach lurched and it felt like the bottom had fallen out of my world. I hadn't been stupid enough to presume we'd get back together but we'd been talking, we'd shared jokes over text and I thought things between us were starting to thaw.

I was on shift but knew I needed some time to get myself together. I prayed a call wouldn't come through and decided to take Kai to the field where I always ran him. I'd had enough.

It was 12.20 a.m. when I got to the field after a short drive on autopilot. I got out and stood by the car with Theo's check chain in my right hand, watching Kai sniff the ground and the cold dark air. Theo's check chain had been Riley's check chain and now it was Kai's. I'd had it my entire career and standing there, watching Kai run, I'd had enough.

I felt utterly broken.

Like I'd lost.

I'd tried my best, but I was broken, beaten. I felt helpless. Now I wanted it all to end. I'd had enough.

If I just hang myself now with this chain …

For a split second, I thought about ending it all. No more pain or hurt, no more confusion, no more work … There was a tree by the edge of the field that would take my weight and I'd done a cadaver course with Sevvy. I knew how quickly it'd be over – it wouldn't take more than a minute for the pain to end, the suffering to be over for good – but I also knew when a body died from hanging other things can happen once the breathing stops. It's not unusual for a hanging suspect to have urinated himself or defecated. I thought about how that might look to whoever found me.

There was a light on the clubhouse on the fire exit that always flashed. It wasn't meant to – the bulb was broken so it didn't flash in time. It'd stay on for a few seconds, then flicker, then off, then on … I didn't look at it, but the irregular illuminations followed my broken thought patterns.

I got in the car and held onto the steering wheel, then got out again and started walking towards the tree. I checked myself and ran back to the car again, shutting and locking the door for a split second before I got out again. Everything felt like it was moving in slow motion and I could hear my pulse in my ears. I didn't want a member of the public finding me, but dog handlers used those woods. It'd be a shock but I knew one of them would be the first to find me in the morning.

As I was contemplating the mechanics of it all, two things flashed through my head: the first was Eryn and Ben, and the second was Theo.

He was at home and no one was coming for him if I ended it.

He'd be waiting for me in the morning.

I felt like I'd let him down by even contemplating ending it. I slumped against the car, crying tears of hurt and relief, squeezing Kai's chain so hard it started to hurt my hand.

Yes, my life wasn't where I wanted it to be. Yes, I was in pain, I'd been let down, I was confused and had a lot to deal with, but who'd let Theo out? He'd spend the rest of his life waiting for me. I couldn't do that to him.

Eryn would be hurt and heartbroken, I knew that, but she was so loved; she had her mum, her grandparents …

Theo had me.

Only me.

I snapped myself out of it but, despite not having moved, I was breathless, my heart pounding in my chest. I was scared by what I'd just thought – I wasn't someone who gave up, I never let go, so how could I even contemplate giving up on my Little Bird and Ben? On Theo, on Kai?

I put a pretty confused Kai back in the car, finished my shift without incident and drove home.

No one at the kennels suspected what had happened and, on the drive home, I vowed I'd fix myself. No matter how long it took, no matter what I had to do, I'd fix things.

Theo's behaviour changed the second I walked through the door, though. While I fussed him, he kept staring at me, like he knew something was up, and from that moment to this he's never, ever far from me. Even as I write these words he's sat under the table, his head resting against my leg. At nights, he'll check on me, putting his wet nose on my cheek, and once I stir he pads back to the landing to sleep. Whether the stress had triggered a chemical change in me he could scent I'll never know, but that night and every night since, he always checks on me – like he knew how close I came to not existing anymore and has made it his purpose to make sure that doesn't happen again.

While negative thoughts over the next couple of days kept trying to push their way into my head, I pushed out all the negatives with positives. I spent a lot of time with Theo, talking to him about everything, unburdening and figuring out a way forward while his head stayed firmly in my lap as I sat on the floor of his kennels with cuppa after cuppa. If he'd been a therapist, it would have cost me a small fortune but he listened for hours while I ran through everything.

I thought about all the things I had – a fantastic daughter and stepson, two dogs who adored me, a rich tapestry of friends all over the country I could rely on, a career I'd forged myself through hard work and determination. I'd been in so many scrapes with Theo and he'd always saved me. Those couple of days were the hardest of my life so far and there he was again, exactly where I needed him to be, doing exactly what I needed without me having to ask or issue a command.

Theo saved me, again.

At the darkest point, those big brown eyes and that torn ear where he'd been bitten were where I needed them to be: right there next to me.

Kai knew something was up, but where Theo would sit quietly and listen, Kai would try and change my mood by bringing me a ball or trying to coax me into a walk by bringing me his lead. He's bonkers at the best of times and his solution always seemed to involve us getting out and about.

20

WITH A HEALTHIER OUTLOOK on the future, I started to enjoy Kai more. We'd been working together a while and I'd spend a lot of our jobs thinking quietly about the fact he wasn't Theo. He didn't do things like Theo and our bond didn't feel like mine and Theo's but, rather than dwell on that as I had been, I started to enjoy Kai for who he was, not who he wasn't.

I threw my energies into my relationship with Eryn even more than I had too, making sure all our time together was quality time. Having struggled mentally myself, I started making sure we chatted through anything that was bothering her at school, something we still do now. She doesn't want to be a dog handler but she helps me with the dogs all the time and her bond with both of them is so strong.

Theo has settled happily into retirement too. He was restless at first and it was hard taking Kai out and leaving him at home but he's been through so much, he's given so much in the line of duty. At first all I could think about was how sad and sorry I was not to be working with him but he's earned his rest. He's taken part in hundreds of arrests and been part of a team that's secured prison sentences. Entire villages and QCs have commended him in court cases. He's not getting any younger, the muzzle is starting to grey a little and he's not as quick as he used to be, but I'm no longer sad he's getting older – he deserves a long and happy life in peace.

A few weeks after I nearly ended everything, Claire asked me for a divorce. It didn't blindside me: I'd thought long and hard about the fact it might be coming shortly after her text saying she'd met someone else and readied myself. While it hurt, that night on the field felt like one chapter ended. Her text asking to make things permanent felt like a new one could finally begin.

There'll always be a massive sadness I couldn't fix us, that I wasn't enough to make us work in the long term, that we couldn't get back what we'd lost, but I can't spend the rest of my life looking back. Accepting my marriage was over will always be a bitter pill to swallow but I learned so much from it and, hand on heart, I wouldn't change any of it. Marrying Claire was the best day of my life, and the love we had when things were good was incredible. I'll always be grateful for it, even if it didn't last as long as I'd wanted it to.

I threw myself into work and Eryn, and was coming off shift in August 2019 when I had a call I wasn't expecting: Sevvy had contracted lungworm. A parasitic infection, it can be fatal. It's carried in slugs and snails and dogs can become infected when they play with or occasionally nibble one. The vet treating him had called because I'd handled him and might want to know. I was told he was unlikely to survive the next twenty-four hours.

When I told Eryn that Sevvy was poorly, she was panicked and worried sick. She was still drawing me pictures of him and talking about him all the time. I phoned the vet's the following morning.

'If you're going to come and see him, do it now because he's going downhill,' I was told.

I decided not to take Eryn with me – I didn't know how bad he was and, when I got there, I was glad I hadn't. He was emaciated, delirious and confused. Seeing Eryn's little Spaniel in such a bad way was devastating and I blamed myself for letting him go.

I'd chosen Theo and now Sevvy was like this.

I knew Eryn would be devastated by how sick he was and the small comfort I had was that she was at home, not beside me. He'd contracted it in Kent, and when I was on shift that day I spoke to the head of the unit. I asked if he pulled through and if he couldn't work again because of the condition, could he be retired to me. I was going through my divorce but I knew if he survived I owed it to him – he was part of my pack.

I'd check on his progress every day and, while they didn't expect him to last the night, Sevvy made it through that one, and the next one, and the next one. Gradually over the course of the next fortnight he started getting stronger. Every single day, Eryn would ask me how he was doing. I hadn't told her how serious it was but she'd draw me pictures to take in to see him. Whether it was his typical Spaniel stubbornness, luck or good fortune I'll never know, but that little dog pulled through and began to get better.

Meanwhile, there were rumours going around the kennels and the unit that his handler was considering promotion, which would mean he wouldn't run Sevvy anymore. It meant the unit would have one body dog and I knew they'd need two. They were trying to canvas the other handlers to see if any of them was interested in training to be a body dog but I was already trained, I knew Sevvy and I seized the opportunity.

I went into my boss and said I knew they needed a body dog handler, and though there were no courses due to start, they knew I could do it. I asked if I could have Sevvy back on a temporary basis until another course started – I knew him, I had trained him and I knew I could get him to work for me again. I made sure I said 'temporary' as much as I could, but I knew I'd never give him back again if he came home. I think the powers that be knew I wanted Sevvy and wouldn't give him back so, while nothing was explicitly agreed in terms of permanence, I knew it was looking hopeful.

On Wednesday, 11 September 2019, I was told I could have Sevvy on a temporary basis. I couldn't get to the kennels fast enough; I felt like a child on Christmas morning. I ran through and dove into his kennel – the quiet little dog I'd seen was as happy as I was.

Our reunion was amazing, but not as beautiful as the one he was about to have …

Eryn was at Claire's mum's house and so I drove straight over. I knocked on the door and Eryn answered.

'I've got a surprise for you, it's in the van …'

I walked her to the back of the van and opened the doors. Eryn stared and stared.

'That's Sevvy!' She started smiling and burst into tears and began squealing with excitement. 'Daddy, you've got Sevvy back!'

They were such tears of joy, pure joy.

I'd delivered, I'd managed to get him back. Sevvy was as excited to see Eryn as she was to see him. She couldn't say thank you enough and I cried as much as she did.

If seeing Eryn and Sevvy reunited was an amazing moment, introducing him back to Theo was the next best thing: Theo was so excited, they played like puppies together.

Within weeks, Sevvy was back working and hadn't lost any of the skills I'd taught him. I had to tell Eryn he was with us on a temporary basis but it soon became apparent he had hearing difficulties as a result of the lungworm, so while I can work him it'll be hard for anyone else to.

My days are good now. If I'm not working, I get Eryn from school. She spends a lot of her time in the house I bought, which I'm slowly doing up; and I was right, she did bound down the stairs the first Christmas she spent here, swinging from the banister and taking the last few steps in one jump. We come home after school and have a snack and do her homework, then Kai gets a rest and we take Theo and Sevvy out for a walk.

If she's at Claire's, I take Theo out for a really long walk. We go up on the moor and I reminisce about the jobs we did and the scrapes we got into. I take him to the pub and sometimes he gets a cheese sandwich from the petrol station if I'm feeling generous.

Kai's becoming a fantastic dog – he's gaining experience and he'll be an epic dog when he comes of age midway through his career just like Theo did.

When working around Manchester, I always remember it for the tracks Theo and I did together. I'm able to look back on my time working Theo with nothing but fondness. There's no sadness or longing to do it again – he's becoming an old man now – but the one regret I have is that I'll never get to see him work again.

I'll work Kai, but I'd give anything to see Theo work again.

If I could have one week of shifts with him again, I'd give everything for it. Between a shift with Theo and a lottery win, I'd choose a night shift on the coldest day in winter with Theo every day. Unless you've been there, unless you've breathed the same air as him on the same track, no words in the world will be able to describe just how awesome he is, just how incredible it was working with him.

In those moments you're one.

ACKNOWLEDGEMENTS

THERE ARE SO MANY PEOPLE I'd like to thank for putting me where I am today and making it possible for me to write this book.

First and foremost, thank you to HarperCollins for this fantastic opportunity and recognition of Theo's achievements and work.

Thank you to the wonderful Clare O'Reilly; always on hand to listen, offer support, keep this project on track and pull together something amazing! Her talent and skill is something she and her family should be very proud of. We met as part of a project and I now regard her as a friend and genuine soul. The world does not have enough people like her.

Thank you to all the police dogs out there who put themselves in danger each and every day in order to protect their handlers and take them home to their families. Thank you for the constant listening and understanding of our complex emotions and moods. Thank you for having the ability to instantly get excited over absolutely nothing, bringing laughter and smiles in sometimes moving times. Thank you for the security and power you bring in the darkest of searches. Without you, the constant fight to bring help and right wrongs would simply be unachievable.

But ultimately, thank you, Theo! Without you none of what I have achieved would have been possible. You are the hero, the legend and the true North. And without you I'd never have had the opportunity to meet who I've met and say, 'Want some orange?' If you know, you know.